# THE WORLD THROUGH MY EYES

# ANDREAS FEININGER

30 YEARS OF PHOTOGRAPHY

# THE WORLD THROUGH MY EYES

CROWN PUBLISHERS, INC., NEW YORK

Acknowledgment

The author and publisher wish to express their sincere thanks to the following corporations, which generously gave their permission to use in this book photographs made by the author that had either been taken for them on assignment or for which author's book *FRAUEN UND GÖTTINNEN*.

*Time, Inc.*, Time and Life Building, New York 20, N. Y., for the use of the photographs which appear on pages 1, 8, 20, 51, 66, 71, 77, 78, 81, 83, 89, 105, 111, 115, 117, 118/119, 122/123, 125, 133, 134/135, 136, 138, 139, 143, 146/147, 148/149, 152/153, 158/159, 161a, 165, 167, 169, 171, which originally were taken on assignments for *Life*.

Prentice-Hall, Inc., Englewood Cliffs, N. J., for the use of several photographs which originally were published in the author's book *THE CREATIVE PHOTOGRAPHER*.
Verlag M. DuMont Schauberg, Köln, Germany, for the use of three photographs which originally were published in the author's book *FRAUEN UND GÖTTINNEN*.

Library of Congress Catalog Card Number: 63-21114
Printed in the Republic of West Germany by
Kleins Druck- und Verlagsanstalt GmbH., Lengerich (Westf.)

# CONTENTS

# BIBLIOGRAPHY

Books written and photographed by Andreas Feiniger

Published in the United States:

"New Paths in Photography," American Photographic Publishing Co., Boston, 1939. (47 photographs and text on the "graphic" control processes, 26 × 29 cm)

"New York," Ziff-Davis Publishing Co., Chicago-New York, 1945. (96 photographs, 27 × 36½ cm)

"Feiniger on Photography," Ziff-Davis Publishing Co., Chicago-New York, 1949. (A study course on the technique and art of photography; 409 pages, illustrated, 21 × 28 cm)

"Advanced Photography," Prentice-Hall, Inc., New York, 1952. (An introduction to creative photography; 244 pages, illustrated, 21 × 28 cm)

"Successful Photography," Prentice-Hall, Inc., Englewood Cliffs, N.J., 1954. (A complete home course in the mechanics, techniques, and applications of photography; 249 pages, illustrated, 15½ × 25½ cm)

"Successful Color Photography," Prentice-Hall, Inc., Englewood Cliffs, N.J., 1954. (A complete home course in the techniques and applications of color photography; 271 pages, illustrated, 15½ × 23½ cm)

"The Face of New York," Crown Publishers, Inc., New York, N.Y., 1954. (168 pages of photographs and text, 22½ × 30½ cm)

"The Creative Photographer," Prentice-Hall, Inc., Englewood Cliffs, N.J., 1955. (Discussions on the creative aspects and practical applications of photography; 329 pages, illustrated, 15½ × 23½ cm

"Changing America," Crown Publishers, Inc., New York, N.Y., 1955. (170 pages of photographs and text, 22½ × 30½ cm)

"The Anatomy of Nature," Crown Publishers, Inc., New York, N.Y., 1956. (168 pages of nature photographs and text, 22½ × 30½ cm)

"Man and Stone," Crown Publishers, Inc., New York, N.Y., 1961. (128 full-page photographs with accompanying text on the stony relics of the past, 26 × 29½ cm)

"Maids, Madonnas, and Witches," Harry N. Abrams, Inc., New York, N.Y., 1961. (143 photographs on the sculpture of the female form, from prehistoric times to Picasso, with accompanying text, 25 × 32½ cm)

"Total Picture Control," Crown Publishers, Inc., New York, N.Y., 1961. (A textbook on the advanced techniques and controls in photography; 351 pages including 271 pages of photographs and captions, 17 × 22½ cm)

Published in Great Britain:

"The Anatomy of Nature," Thomas Yoseloff Ltd., London. (The British edition of "The Anatomy of Nature")

"The Image of Woman," Thames and Hudson, London, 1961. (The British edition of "Maids, Madonnas, and Witches")

"A Manual of Advanced Photography," Thames and Hudson, London, 1962. (The British edition of "Total Picture Control")

Published in Germany:

"Menschen vor der Kamera," Heering-Verlag, Harzburg, 1934. (A manual on portrait photography and the photography of people; 176 pages, illustrated)

"Selbst Entwickeln und Kopieren," Heering-Verlag, Harzburg, 1935. (A textbook on developing and printing; 136 pages)

"Vergrößern leicht gemacht," Heering-Verlag, Harzburg, 1936. (A textbook on enlarging; 168 pages, illustrated)

"Fotografische Gestaltung," Heering-Verlag, Harzburg, 1937. (A book on the creative aspects of photography; 152 pages including 48 pages of illustrations)

"Das Antlitz der Natur," Droemersche Verlagsanstalt Th. Knaur Nachf., München-Zürich, 1957. (The German edition of "The Anatomy of Nature")

"Das Buch der Fotografie," Econ-Verlag, Düsseldorf, 1959. (The German edition of "Successful Photography")

"Der Schlüssel zur Fotografie von heute," Econ-Verlag, Düsseldorf, 1953. (The German edition of "The Creative Photographer")

"Das Buch der Farb-Fotografie," Econ-Verlag, Düsseldorf, 1959. (The German edition of "Successful Color Photography")

"Feininger fotografiert Steine," Econ-Verlag, Düsseldorf, 1960. (The German edition of "Man and Stone")

"Frauen und Göttinnen," Verlag M. DuMont Schauberg, Köln, 1960. (The German edition of "Maids, Madonnas, and Witches")

"Die Hohe Schule der Fotografie," Econ-Verlag, Düsseldorf, 1961. (The German edition of "Total Picture Control")

Published in Sweden:

"Stockholm," Albert Bonniers Förlag, Stockholm, 1963. (A picture book on Stockholm; 121 pages of photographs, 26 × 25 cm)

"Framgångsrik fotografering," Bonniers, Stockholm. (The Swedish edition of "Successful Photography")

"Framgångsrik färg fotografering," Bonniers, Stockholm. (The Swedish edition of "Successful Color Photography")

"Skapande fotografering," Bonniers, Stockholm. (The Swedish edition of "The Creative Photographer")

Published in Finland:

"Hyvä Valokuvaaja," Tammi, Helsinki, 1957. (The Finnish edition of "Successful Photography")

"Värivalokuvaaja," Tammi, Helsinki, 1958. (The Finnish edition of "Successful Color Photography")

Published in Danmark:

"Feiningers Fotoskole," Grafisk Forlag, Kopenhagen, 1962. (The Danish edition of "Total Picture Control")

Published in Italy:

"Il libro della fotografia," Garzanti, Milano, 1961. (The Italian edition of "Successful Photography")

"Il libro della fotografia a colori," Garzanti, Milano, 1962. (The Italian edition of "Successful Color Photography")

Published in Holland:

"Vorm en functie in de natuur," W. Gaade N. V., Delft (The Dutch edition of "The Anatomy of Nature")

Published in Spain:

"Anatomia de la Naturaleza," Editorial Jano, Barcelona, 1962. (The Spanish edition of "The Anatomy of Nature")

Published in France:

"Voir en photographie," Edita, Lausanne, 1963. (The French edition of "The Creative Photographer")

# INTRODUCTION

Pictures cover every available space in my work-room—the walls, the floor, chairs, tabletops. They are placed for review: a selection from the accumulation of twenty-five years, spread out so that I can examine what I have done during that time. I want to see how far I succeeded in conveying my own feeling about a subject, in presenting an idea.

No one can evaluate his own work with complete objectivity, no matter how honest his intention. But one tries. And faced with this massive collection of prints, I asked myself a question: Have I fulfilled what I set out to do, and if so, has my initial intention not only been present but present in an aesthetic frame? Are the pictures striking enough that, seen again in such number, they still are interesting? Are they sufficiently interesting that the observer, finding some new appreciation through them and remembering them, is made more aware or more thoughtful?

And looking at these pictures, I considered these things and thought about my beginnings as a photographer and what had made me choose photography as a profession.

In my youth I dreamed of becoming a scientist. I roamed the fields and woods surrounding my home town, observing and collecting animals and plants, wishing I could record them in their natural habitat. One Christmas I was given a camera. The first photograph I ever made was of crows feeding in a snow-covered field. In the print, the crows appeared as specks, so great was the distance between them and me. Perhaps it was this first failure to get the image I had imagined that accounted for my later interest in tele- and close-up photography.

When circumstances prevented me from pursuing a scientific career I became an architect. In the course of my studies I saw many buildings, constructions, and structural details that appealed to me. At first I started to sketch these, but I soon found that sketching was too slow and inaccurate. Instead, I began to photograph them, and I discovered the camera was an ideal means by which to compile a pictorial reference library of my own.

The political upheaval of the mid-thirties (I lived in Europe at that time) made it impossible for me to continue my career as an architect, and so I became an architectural photographer. Now I found myself taking pictures for other architects and the editors of architectural magazines.

When World War II began, I came to the United States and was fortunate enough to become a

*Life* photographer. With that, the most exciting period of my career began. In working for *Life,* the thrill of traveling, meeting interesting people, getting into places barred to most others, and seeing things that I could not otherwise have seen at first hand was just as great as that of the photographic work. I was in the enviable position of doing what pleased me most and being paid for it by the magazine. And since my assignment editor, Wilson Hicks, was very much aware that any photographer does his best work if a subject has interest for him, most of my assignments involved things I loved—the objects and forms of nature, and the works of man.

Paradoxical as it may sound, I ascribe whatever success I have had in photography to the fact that my greatest interest has always been in the subjects of my pictures, not in photographic equipment and technique. In fact, I was so little concerned by the mechanics of picture-making that I never bothered to learn in the approved manner by being apprenticed to a photographer or by attending a photo school. Instead, I carefully read and conscientiously tried to follow the instructions that accompanied any camera, film, or developer I bought. Of course, I made mistakes I might have avoided if I had had proper guidance.

However, being a perfectionist by nature, when I was dissatisfied with what I had produced, I stubbornly looked for the cause of the trouble, and if I succeeded in finding it, I rarely made the same mistake again. As a result of this self-education, I acquired a thorough understanding of the entire photographic process which I doubt I would have obtained by any other method.

Interest in a subject gives the necessary spark that is required for anyone's best work. It is interest that stimulates the desire to explore one's theme, and it is in such exploration that a photographer often makes unexpected discoveries or gains the insight without which he could not have made a meaningful photograph.

Part of the reward one receives for his work is the knowledge that it will be seen and appreciated by others; part of its meaning is the meaning beyond oneself. And photography provides a universal method of communication, breaking through the barriers of language so easily that no barriers seem to exist. At this perilous time in our world, communication and understanding are vitally important, so photography should rank high as an avenue of international intercourse.

To me, the camera is a tool that serves many purposes. It is there when I find subjects which I am compelled to photograph—to record them for my own study or enjoyment; it is there when I want to photograph for others what has appealed to me, so that I can share what I think important or beautiful.

Though the approach of photographers may range from the objective to the subjective, and their pictures appear very different, good pictures have at least one common factor—interest. The way in which each photographer chooses to work is almost always determined by his interest.

In the objective approach, the photographer tries to efface himself, to record the subject as faithfully as possible, presenting it to the observer for his own interpretation. This is the approach of the scientist or documentarian. It is the technique I most often follow. Two others who have used this approach at its highest level are Cartier-Bresson and Edward Weston.

In the subjective approach, a photographer's feelings are engaged. He wants us to be drawn by his own reaction, to feel as he felt. If his insight and creative ability are of a high order, he catches us in his net. We see as he has seen, in the depicted intensity of his own vision. And once caught, we are not captive, but released spontaneously to a wider view. Erwin Blumenfeld, Ernst Haas, and Gordon Parks are, in my opinion, outstanding photographers who follow a subjective approach in their work.

This, I think, is the greatest difference between the two approaches: In the first, the viewer's reaction is unprompted and he is thrown back to his own experience for reference. In the second, he is propelled toward the reaction of the photographer.

As I have already said, I use the objective rather than the subjective approach to photography. I am fortunate enough to have a talent for analysis and organization, and I am primarily an observer. Since my mind inclines toward the scientific, my approach, as a result, is more intellectual than emotional. These qualities are, of course, reflected in my selection of subjects and in the form of their rendition.

Subjects I am most interested in primarily involve fact rather than feeling: the documentation of things rather than emotions. These subjects include manifestations of nature—rocks, plants, and animals in all their infinite variations—and the works of man. What interests me most in these subjects are the aspects of structure, function, and form. There is a functional beauty in all natural forms, and I feel strongly that only when man-made forms are related to their functions can the result be aesthetically satisfying.

Since I am primarily concerned with function and form, factors such as sharpness, contrast, and simplicity of composition are important to my work. However, though my own work puts emphasis upon these qualities, I greatly admire certain other photographers' work that depends upon the use of softness and blur to express the intangibles of feeling and mood.

I believe that to accomplish anything worthwhile one must know and accept one's limitations and reject the temptation to exceed one's scope. Those who allow admiration for others' work to carry them beyond their own capacities no longer produce original work; they become mere imitators. Within one's own limitations, a personal style can be evolved through choice of subject and technique of rendition. The number of subjects to be photographed is limitless and the techniques of rendering are many. To encompass them all is impossible, and one must make a choice. Since no two people are alike, differences in personality will influence this choice. In following one's own way and pursuing one's own interests against the pressures and temptations to do otherwise, each finds his style. The discipline and dedication exacted in doing

this, however, are so great that those who arrive at a highly personal style are few in relation to the total number of photographers. And fewer still are those whose talents are such that they create, through experiment in visual representation, a whole new way of seeing things. These few photographers, through their innovations, better the work of others and contribute to the advance of photography. And though their imitators may unfortunately be many, their own force is not canceled. Some of the photographers whom I admire and who have influenced my own thinking and work through their creativity are Erwin Blumenfeld, Ernst Haas, Gjon Mili, Laszlo Moholy-Nagy, Albert Renger-Patzsch, Eliot Porter, Man Ray, Emil Schulthess, W. Eugene Smith, and Edward Weston.

Each of these, dissatisfied with the accepted forms and rules of photographic expression, boldly struck out on his own. Each used existing but generally overlooked means and techniques to show familiar subjects in different ways, thereby making the observer aware of things that previously had escaped his attention or thought. In this way, each of these photographers created a powerful personal style.

When a photographer lacks a personal style, it is usually either because he is unimaginative or because he hasn't "found himself." As long as he is addicted to following the advice of others or is floundering in imitation, he cannot work out a style of his own.

What personal style I possess springs from a definite concept of the purpose of photography—of a "philosophy" which, briefly expressed, is this: Photography is a picture-language. Through it a photographer can communicate his ideas or feelings about people, events, or things.

To fulfill that purpose, a photograph must interest those for whom it is meant and must be presented in a form that the observer can understand.

The photographer's own true interest in his subject is very likely to call forth response in others. And if he has fully explored the possibilities of his subject, his picture is bound to appeal to others, for they will be caught by thought associations or similarity of feeling. Hundreds—thousands—of amateur photographers are proof of this in reverse: Free to spend their time in photographing things unassigned, with a chance to state their own ideas and express themselves completely, they instead endlessly take the most uninteresting subjects in stereotyped form, with the result that their pictures call forth no response in others. I am convinced that the work of many photographers would be tremendously improved if they restricted themselves to subjects in which they were really interested and photographed these for the sake of communication rather than merely to produce pictures.

Though the subject is of primary importance, inseparable from it is the form in which it is rendered. To decide upon the way in which a subject should be rendered—or translated—from reality into picture form is considerably more difficult than it may seem at first because a photograph is *not* a realistic reproduction, but a semi-abstract rendition, of a subject. In consequence, its effect depends upon the use of symbols.

In photography, three-dimensional subjects must be rendered in two dimensions; motion must be expressed in a "still"; and in black-and-white renditions, color must be translated into shades of gray. Therefore, in this medium in which depth, motion, and color can only be suggested, symbols must be used, and only if they are selected and applied with skill and sensitivity will a photograph be good or excellent.

Anyone can take a recognizable picture of almost any subject, but there is a great difference between a merely recognizable and a truly effective rendition of the same subject. And whether a photograph falls into one category or the other is dependent upon the photographer's particular use of symbols.

There are many symbols that can be used to suggest those qualities that cannot be rendered directly. Depth can be symbolized by perspective: apparent converging of receding parallel lines, and apparent diminution in size; foreshortening of form and overlapping of objects; by contrast between sharp and unsharp; or contrast between light and dark; and through composition. Motion can be symbolized by blur; multiple exposure or multiple printing; time exposure; panning; picture sequences; and through composition. And color can be symbolized by controlled contrast and graphically effective black and white. Symbols can furthermore be used to suggest intangibles: lightness and darkness, to suggest feeling or mood; graininess, to create emphasis through texture; halation, to give the intensity of light; and so forth.

Any subject or event can be photographed or presented in picture form in many different ways. Every change in distance; angle of view; focal length, angle, and coverage of the lens; speed, color-sensitivity, and graininess of the film; plane of focus; diaphragm aperture; filter color; film ex-

posure; method of development; contrast of the printing paper; exposure, dodging, and cropping of the print; and every change in any one of a multitude of other factors will produce differences through combinations that are innumerable. Cartier-Bresson has had interesting things to say on the technique of catching the precise instant. Thorough knowledge of all these factors and techniques is required to express precisely what one wishes to communicate.

A good photograph, I think, is one which conveys to the observer something that he has not seen, known, or thought of before; in other words, a photograph which is "new" to him, insofar as it stimulates his imagination, increases his knowledge, or enriches him aesthetically, intellectually, or emotionally.

This demands a great deal from the photographer. The kind of newness I have in mind is that which results from an original approach or from an innovation—a new way of seeing or rendering a subject; that which proves to be the successful end of a search for a new way of expression; that which extends the artist's vision; that which the creative photographer seeks and finds; and, finally, that which the photographer is able to extract from the seemingly implacable structure of technique to convey what he wishes to say. For in creative hands, the camera, like the telescope and the microscope, becomes an instrument to widen man's horizons—providing greater knowledge, understanding, and insight.

This kind of newness demands a thorough comprehension of the characteristics of the photographic medium and a utilization of those qualities that belong to no other. In the following, I shall give only an abbreviated account of these typically photographic qualities, which are more fully discussed in my book *The Creative Photographer*.

### Authenticity

—A photograph is a document, an eyewitness account of a subject or an event. The quality of authenticity gives a photograph a power of conviction not associated with any other medium of communication. Since this quality is inherent in the photographic process, awareness of it should make one consider first whether a subject is worth recording.

### Accuracy of drawing

—another unique quality of the photographic medium, can be maintained throughout a picture, down to the rendition of the most minute detail.

This quality often goes unused where it would have been valuable, because some photographers think sharpness is alien to "art." For my part, I have no objection to the use of *un*sharpness—it is a very useful technique, and when correctly employed creates remarkable effects. But sharpness makes it possible for us to see reality with greater accuracy in photographic images than we could otherwise see it, and so this characteristic should be fully exploited to make us more aware of the wondrous aspects of our world.

### Speed of recording

—a third unique property of photography. In an instant the image of a subject or event is permanently recorded. If an equivalent impression were to be written or painted, it might require hours, days, or even weeks.

However, though immensely valuable, speed of recording involves certain dangers. The most obvious is the thoughtless snapping of many pictures of the same subject in rapid succession, in the hope that one will prove a hit. This machine-gun approach is usually futile as well as costly.

### Polychrome into monochrome

—The translation of color into shades of gray may appear to be a poor substitute for natural color, if one thinks of it only in that context. That monochrome renditions were done in other media ages before photography was invented makes monochrome in photography seem not so strange. Actually, black-and-white photography provides an easy solution to the problem of translating natural color into a semiabstract form while simultaneously preserving its tone and contrast values. And monochrome renditions cannot be replaced by renditions in color. The different—and desirable—characteristics of the two insure the continuance of both, as in other media. Not only artists but most well-known photographers work in black and white as well as color, choosing one or the other as the subject demands.

The main advantage of working in black and white is that the rendition is simplified. Color is frequently a distracting element in a picture, and its absence often allows for greater emphasis upon such essentials as space, light, form, outline, and texture. Unless color is essential to the characterization of a subject, it need not be used. And as far as graphic impact is concerned, nothing provides it so well as areas of pure black and white.

*From the nearest to the farthest*
—The range of vision of the human eye, compared to that of the camera, is very limited indeed. Objects closer than approximately eight inches are seen indistinctly or not at all by the normal eye. Remote objects are seen in correspondingly less detail as their distance becomes greater. However, distance or closeness present no problem in photography, for the great variety of lenses of different focal lengths makes it possible to produce large, clear images of objects at distances from fractions of an inch to infinity. Thus, photography can extend our knowledge of the world, showing us things once unknown because they were too small or too far away to be seen. Exploring our surroundings through close-up and telephoto lenses—which can bring into focus anything from microbes to mountains on the moon—has always seemed a fascinating aspect of photography to me, and much of my work has been along these lines.

*From narrow to ultra-wide angle of view*
—The angle of view of the human eye is fixed, but the camera can enlarge its vision to 180 degrees: one half of the visible world can be shown in a single photograph. The perspective of such super wide-angle photographs is not rectilinear but spherical. In such photographs,

though reality is, through change in perspective, so unlike what we naturally see, nevertheless the relationship of objects to their suroundings is given a new clarity. The potentiality of greatly widening our visual experience through work in this field is, I think, immense. As far as I know, only Bill Brandt and Emil Schulthess have attempted to exploit it.

*Ability to record motion*
—Photography can record objects in motion as the eye cannot see them in reality. In picture form, we can "freeze" motion, thus making visible things whose speed is too rapid to register on the retina; or, through time exposures, record in one photograph the progress of a subject's motion and thereby produce veritable graphs of space and time. These techniques also, by showing something that otherwise could not be seen, add to our understanding and enjoyment of our world.

*Multiple images*
—The eye cannot properly perceive a rapidly moving object; neither can it combine successive images into one. In the photographic medium both these things can be done with ease, and through multiple exposure or multiple printing we can re-

solve motion into phases which, sharply rendered and superimposed, express movement with an entirely new clarity, fluidity, and beauty of form.

*Light-accumulating ability*
—The dimmer the light, the less we see. Photographic emulsions, however, are not subject to this limitation. Light sources too dim to be perceptible can, through extended exposure and the resulting accumulation of light, produce a usable image on film. This quality can be of vital importance—for example, in the study of the universe. It makes it possible for astronomers to record the ghostly images of galaxies so remote that no telescope has yet been able to make them directly visible to the eye.

*Positive and negative*
—Photography provides the only simple, accurate, and automatic means for changing positive images into negative ones. It seems to me that inherent in negative prints are many possibilities for graphic expression that merit closer attention by creative photographers.
Negative prints are still little known and therefore they invariably intrigue the observer. That they are more abstract than positive black-and-

white prints makes them particulary suitable for the presentation of abstract concepts and themes. And the graphic effect of a negative print is, as a rule, stronger than that of its positive counterpart, especially if the contrast is high. An interesting technique, particularly for semiabstract renditions, consists of printing a negative, superimposed but slightly off register, in conjunction with the corresponding positive transparency, to make a "bas-relief" print.

## Isolation and concentration

—The eye does not completely isolate a part of reality from its surroundings. The camera does, and unless care is taken, a photograph may appear not as whole but as a fragment, aesthetically unsatisfactory, difficult or impossible to understand. However, when the isolation is successful, that selected part of reality can make a stronger impression upon us than the actual subject because it has been freed from the distracting elements of its surroundings.

If a photograph is to be succesfulness as far as isolation of the subject is concerned, it must be a self-contained unit. Among other things, it must have only one theme and this theme must be rendered in a form that is simple, clear, and free of nonessential

detail. Regardless of the subject, the picture must be so organized that the balance of black and white, contrast, line, outline, and form contribute to a graphically interesting pattern, and the proportions of the print must be compatible with the character of the subject. In short, the same principles that govern other forms of graphic art also govern photography.

## From X-ray to radiant heat

—The human eye is sensitive to only a narrow band of the electromagnetic spectrum, but photographic emulsions can be sensitized to a much wider range of waves, from the very short X-rays through ultraviolet and visible light to long-wave infrared radiation and radiant heat. These forms of radiation possess properties that, utilized photographically, make it possible for us to depict things we cannot see in any other way.

Photography of this kind is of incalculable worth in research in astronomy, physics, medicine, and engineering. And on other levels, it is used in long-distance, tele-, and aerial photography, in the authentication of old masters, in criminal investigations, the exposure of forgeries, and in other fields. These twelve photographic characteristics, when used with skill and imagination, permit the photographer to bring to the observer's attention aspects of a subject or event that otherwise might have escaped his notice. This is possible because the camera can "see" reality in a more penetrating way than the eye. Thus, pictures that show what the eye, unaided, cannot see, arouse a feeling of surprise and discovery that makes them far more interesting than a literal photograph. I have been aware of the importance of these reactions of discovery and surprise ever since I began to take photography seriously and as far as possible have deliberately tried to produce pictures that will evoke such a response in the observer.

To express his ideas or feelings effectively—to show a subject as he wishes it to be seen—a photographer must have technical skill with the tools of his trade. Good technique is fundamental to our craft. To attain it involves practice, practice, and more practice—learning from trial and error. The only way to perfection is through endless experiment. Try this, try that, repeat, improve, then try again. This is what I have done to correct my mistakes. Gradually and systematically, I have investigated and analyzed just about every aspect of photographic rendition, saving all the results of my experiments, whether they were successful or not. Through this kind of training I learned how

to translate my concepts and ideas into graphic form, to put them down on film and paper as shown in the photographs of this book.

Speaking of photo-technique, I know that each photographer has his own ideas regarding its importance to the making of good photographs. Opinion ranges from a conviction that excellence of technique is vitally important, to the belief that preoccupation with photo-technical problems acts as a barrier to spontaneous, creative picture-taking. Fortunately, there is no hard and fast rule. Though I find a complete command of technique essential to my own way of working, I greatly admire the work of some photographers who have only the barest rudiments of "technical" knowledge. On the other hand, there are photographers who are so completely engrossed in technical facts and theories that their pictures lack everything else.

In some respects, preoccupation with the technical side of photography can put obstacles in the path of making good photographs. I have seen photographers miss what Cartier-Bresson calls "the decisive moment" while they worry about light-meter readings and length of exposure. Some photographers "know too much" about technique. Burdened by what they think can or cannot be done, they often pass up unusual pictures as impossible to capture successfully. They will not risk shooting into a brilliant light, or take a picture if there is much movement of the subject or the camera, or if a shutter speed is so slow as to invite motion of the hand-held camera; if the light seems too weak, or the contrast too high, they miss their opportunities forever. And yet, even though it may be impossible to get technically perfect photographs (in the academic sense) under such conditions, sometimes seemingly unfavorable conditions do yield impressive and captivating pictures, as can be seen in innumerable photographs in *Paris-Match* and *Life*.

Once this preoccupation with technique has taken hold, it spreads to the whole process: films are tested to determine the one with the finest grain, the highest resolution and speed; developers are tested for their ability to reduce grain; papers are tested to see which yields the richest black and the longest gradation of tones. The differences are often so minute that if they are to be seen at all, samples must be compared side by side under high magnification or in a strong light. And if one's work is for publication, these slight variations are canceled out when the photograph is printed in a magazine or book because the screen of the en-graving and printing processes obliterates any technical advantage of this kind. Time, energy, and money that could have been invested to better ends have been wasted.

The technical perfection of a picture, of course, should be as great as possible, but different types of photographs should be judged by standards that take into account the conditions under which each was made, rather than by a single standard for all. It is useless to demand that an action shot taken with a 35-mm camera in very poor light measure up to the technical excellence that can be achieved in a situation that presents no problems. To evaluate a photograph technically without considering the conditions under which it was made, or without regard for the possibility that photo-technical manifestations normally considered faults (like grain, blur, or halation) may have been used deliberately to create specific effects, is not to understand the medium.

Photo-technique is rooted in one's own standards and in the requirements and latitude defined by the subject. Since I am interested primarily in subjects that neither move nor change quickly, I work mostly with large cameras. Although cumbersome and slow in performance, they produce negatives far superior in technical excellence. During my twenty-five years as a professional photographer I have owned cameras ranging in size from 35 mm to 8 × 10 inches. Invariably, I have found that I produced the best results in black and white when I used a 4 × 5, and in color a 5 × 7, because they were best suited not only to the kind of subject I most often photograph but to my temperament and ways of working too.

I like to work slowly and deliberately, taking time to be sure that everything is correct. This devotion to perfection has more than once muted spontaneity, lessening that essential part of creativity that gives a picture its life. However, it is useless to go against one's temperament. I have tried that and then there was no joy in my work.

At the time of this writing I own two Plaubel 4 × 5-inch view cameras—a Peco Supra II, which I use mostly at home and in the studio, and a Peco Junior, which I use when I travel; a 5 × 7 thirty-year-old Linhof Technika, which I use exclusively for color; two Rolleiflexes (all the photographs in my book *Man and Stone* were taken with an eighteen-year-old Rolleiflex); a Hasselblad, which I find particularly good for close-up and telephotography; and a Heiland Pentax, which I use almost exclusively for color. I have lenses of different focal lengths for all these cameras with the exception, of course, of the Rolleis. To simplify equipment and save weight and bulk when I travel, I modified the fronts of the 4 × 5 and 5 × 7 cameras so that all three accept the standard 4 × 4-inch lens boards on which all my large-camera lenses are mounted; and through use of a simple adapter I can use my Hasselblad lenses on the Pentax.

Although I always print my black-and-white negatives myself, a first-class commercial laboratory develops all my films, both color and black-and-white, and has done so for many years. Their automatic equipment and processing in deep tanks with nitrogen-burst agitation produces much more uniform development than I could with small tanks and manual agitation. However, when it comes to enlarging the negatives, I always do that myself, except for duplicate prints made by a technician using my print as a guide. The photographer himself is the only one who can know precisely what he wants in his prints. Feeling, mood, degree of contrast, distribution of light and dark areas controlled by dodging, sectional enlarging of specific negative areas, and cropping of the print to the right proportions can be executed properly by no one else. Photographers who do not enlarge their own negatives relinquish a very important step in a process that enormously influences the effect of their pictures.

In the twenty-one years that I worked for *Life* I had some 350 assignments, from single pictures to full-length essays that took months to complete and ran up to nineteen pages in the magazine. During these years I traveled widely, covering subject matter on themes ranging from "National Purpose" and "Push-Button Defense for Air War" to "Art Riches of the Andes", and "The World of the Insects." I have watched the deserts of the West bloom miraculously when spring came, and have seen how and where men dig to find uranium. I did a story on the Adams papers, another on the melting and making of glass, a third one on steel, and I have walked and watched and photographed on the piers and the many streets of the city where I live, New York. I have photographed the inauguration of a President of the United States, Congress in action, and a mosquito in the act of biting; coal mines and Coney Island at night; a white python—and the glaciers of the Canadian Northwest. And these are but a fraction of the things I have seen.

This variety of subjects gives an idea of the demands made upon a *Life* photographer. He must be able to cope with such differing surroundings as the laboratory of a nuclear physicist, the Capitol of the United States, a coal mine, the slums of Chicago (which, I believe, are the world's worst). He must get along with people and be able to enlist their cooperation, whatever their position or learning. And no matter what he is assigned to photograph, whether it is a super close-up of an insect or a tele-view of an entire city, he must, of course, be able to show it in a picture form that gains the attention of the reader. The range of a *Life* photographer's assignments is so great it provides an education that is wide, fascinating, and unique.

It has always bothered me that the work my colleagues and I did for *Life* was so short-lived—lasting, as a rule, only through the week of the magazine's sale. Among these pictures are, I think, many of lasting value—time-bound stories of historical importance and timeless pictures that can be seen again and again, as good paintings and sculpture are seen and enjoyed. It was in the hope of saving some of these pictures from oblivion that I began to do picture books.

Years ago, in 1934, I first tried my hand at writing, and produced a series of photo-technical instruction books for Heering Verlag in Germany. Subsequently, I made a picture book of Stockholm, Sweden, which was published in 1936 by Albert Bonniers Förlag in Stockholm. The Stockholm book presented an interesting problem. This city is a seaport built partly on islands, and the great cruise ships anchor in its heart. The best views, across water, presented a problem in distance which could not be solved with a lens of standard focal length. I could not afford the proper equipment at that time, so I set about building my own tele-camera. It consisted of two wooden boxes of rectangular cross-section, one slightly smaller than the other so that it could be slid back and forth for focusing. The contraption had as its lens the front element of an old French Rapid Aplanat. The focal length was approximately 20 inches, and when stopped down to $f/32$, it sharply covered a $6 \times 9$-cm negative. This lens had no shutter, and so I had to expose my films by using the lens cap. To cut the haze and prolong exposure times to manageable values, I used a dark red filter.

A great reward was inherent in the making of this primitive though adequate camera: I learned a good deal about telephotography, particularly how to eliminate the camera vibration caused by long extensions of the "bellows." My experience with this camera eventually led me to design my present 40-inch telephoto camera and its supporting "five-pod."

To photograph a subject in a particular way, I have often needed equipment that was either unavailable or too expensive, and in such cases I built the equipment myself from simple parts and wood. It was usually not too difficult to do, and I had great fun doing it. Among the things I built are four different telephoto cameras, each a refinement of a previous model; two enlargers, each one equipped with banks of individually controllable lights used in dodging and fitted with negative carriers that could be tilted for perspective control; various types of vibration-free supports for telephoto cameras; extension bellows for both large and small cameras, exposure-calibrated for super close-ups; a semiautomatic diaphragm control based upon a ring and a pin; and a number of devices for producing star-patterns and other symbols to suggest the radiance of brilliant light. If one were to spend time doing this today he might be considered slightly mad, but twenty years ago when I made most of these things, very few of them existed and those that did were beyond my means. Besides, it is not only fun to make such things but also extremely instructive, for in the making one gains an understanding of the principles involved and thereby the potentialities of the equipment. Such understanding leads to the making of better photographs. For this reason, I recommend that a photographer build a part of his equipment himself, even if he can afford to buy everything he needs.

By the time I had worked some ten years for *Life* I had gained so much experience, collected so much data, and learned so many interesting facts that I felt the desire to share my knowledge with others. In this, I was greatly encouraged by Wilson Hicks, then *Life's* picture editor. As a result, I wrote *Feininger on Photography*, which was not only concerned with the technical problems of the medium, but also included my experiences with—and ideas in relation to—the creative

aspects of photography. Subsequently to keep pace with the advances in photo-technology, I wrote five other textbooks, and to keep those of my photographs which I thought of value from being buried in files, I continued to produce picture books.

In this book are the pictures I consider the most significant of all those I spread out in my workroom for review. With them, I shall include some of my thoughts on pictures and picture-making, stressing my ideas on technique and discussing various aspects of photography and the different approaches to and requirements of each—things that I have learned and conclusions I have arrived at during some thirty years of photographic work.

# I

*The Element of Surprise*

I have always had a great deal of curiosity. Thanks to it, I have derived great pleasure from looking at and studying the things that make up my environment, trying to understand their nature and function, their origin and subsequent change. A large part of a photographers's life is necessarily spent in waiting—for an assignment, for permission to photograph a particular subject, for the right kind of weather or conditions to prevail. Such delays are burdensome if spent in passive waiting, but enjoyable if one considers himself, not imprisoned, but unexpectedly released to indulge his curiosity—to read a book, to go to a museum, an exhibition, or a gallery, to track down some interesting fact, to watch a hornet queen build her nest, or to walk in the woods, marveling at the endless complexity of life.

To a person who has as much curiosity as I, the camera is an instrument with limitless potentialities, an eye capable of showing things the human eye is too limited to see. Used with love and patience—sometimes even in relatively unskilled hands—the camera can satisfy to an unexpected degree our curiosity about people and things, depicting them with an intensity of seeing that is a constant source of pleasure, revealing characteristics, details, or facts that we have not seen, known, or thought of before. The quality of surprise—the depicting of the unexpected—lends interest to a photograph. Almost any kind of subject, I believe, can be photographed in such a way that it will have this quality, and even familiar and often-photographed subjects can be shown in new and interesting forms.

The following four pictures seem to me to illustrate this fact.

## 1. A navy rescue helicopter takes off at night

The luminous spiral so delicately etched against the sky was traced by two small lamps mounted at the tips of the helicopter's rotor for the purpose of attracting the attention of those in distress at sea. A publicity shot of the helicopter had appeared in the daily newspapers, but the light track was shapeless because the helicopter was photographed as it went vertically up and down several times. A *Life* editor saw that shot and asked me to improve on it. I planned my picture carefully, even to considering the position of the moon. Then I asked the helicopter pilot to follow a path which, I thought, would give the best result: a straight ascent, a forward slip, then a right-angle turn, and finally a gradual climb that would carry the aircraft directly over my head. The surprise in this photograph is seeing the total flight pattern—something we cannot see in this form in actuality—as a design that is aesthetically pleasing, a graph of motion and time.

After two rehearsal flights during which I checked the flight pattern on the groundglass, I made this shot with a 4 × 5-inch view camera mounted on a tripod, using a 9-cm Angulon wide-angle lens stopped down to approximately $f/16$, Kodak Super-XX film pack, and a time exposure that lasted as long as the helicopter was within the field of view of the lens.

## 2. A wolf spider killing a grasshopper

Here we see murder on a miniature scale, the dramatic end of the life of a grasshopper overpowered by a spider. A life-and-death struggle of this kind occurs on a scale too small to be noticed normally, and much too small to be followed in detail by the unaided eye. Again, the camera reaches beyond the inadequacies of our vision by magnifying the participants in the drama to a scale that makes everything clearly visible, including seven of the spider's eight eyes.

This photograph was made with a Hasselblad $2\frac{1}{4} \times 2\frac{1}{2}$ inches, equipped with homemade extension bellows, on Kodak Super-XX rollfilm; in substitution for the totally inadequate natural light, a single flashbulb on an extension was held high to give a combination of overhead light and backlight. The scale of magnification in the reproduction is approximately twelve times linear natural size.

### 3. Worker in an auto body paint shop

This is not a portrait of a Martian but of a man wearing a gas mask. Here I used the camera to emphasize the fantastic aspects of the equipment—the goggling eyes, the synthetic nose, the filter snout—picked out in harsh, dramatic black and white. The startling effect was achieved through the use of light and by very close cropping, which eliminated everything that did not contribute to the planned impression.

A Rolleiflex shot made in the harsh glare of an industrial overhead lamp (deliberately not softened by shadow fill-in) produced a strong, graphic black-and-white quality in the print.

### 4/5. Midtown Manhattan at 42nd Street seen from across the Hudson

An attempt to capture the feeling of superhuman scale, even the monstrosity, of a modern metropolis. The effect of this photograph is derived primarily from maintaining the actual scale: in comparison to the usual photograph—in which, through perspective diminution, small objects close to the camera appear much larger than remote but actually very large objects, which seem unnaturally small—the proportions in this picture are reversed. That is, relatively small objects located in the foreground are rendered small in relation to the large buildings in the background, which, despite their great distance from the camera, actually dominate the scene.

This kind of perspective, in which diminution is held to a minimum, renders the picture elements in more or less their true proportions—frees the picture from the falsification that would be imposed upon its scale by foreshortening and diminution—and although such a picture does not exactly conform to what we see in reality, nevertheless it conveys to the highest degree the feeling of dominance and brute power that the skyscrapers of Manhattan evoke at first sight.

I was able to achieve this type of perspective by using an extreme telephoto lens and making the picture from a great distance. The shoreline is approximately two miles away from the place where I made the photograph, and the farthest buildings five miles. The camera used was a 4 × 5-inch telecamera of my own design, equipped with an old Dallmeyer Grandac lens with a focal length of 40 inches.

▮▶

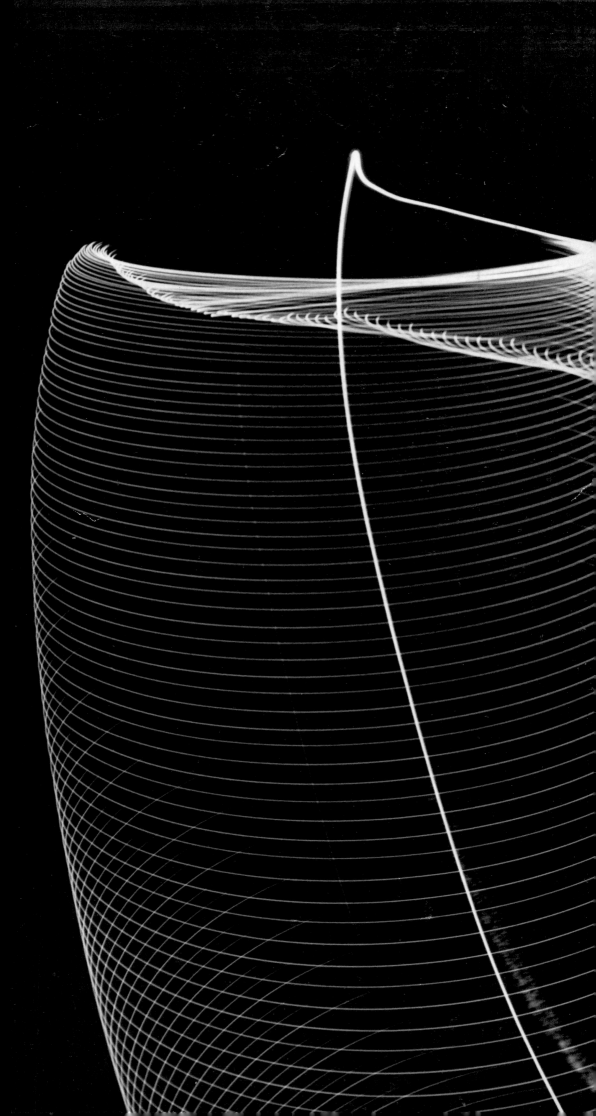

# II

## The Precise Image

I find the almost incredible precision with which a sharp lens can render the subjects I photograph an endless source of enjoyment. To me, precision is a truly "modern" quality—a quality that in this degree of perfection was unknown to previous generations, although the copper and steel engravers of the eighteenth and nineteeth centuries came fairly close to producing it; a quality that today exists to an almost unbelievable degree of perfection in fine microscopes and astronomical telescopes, rocket guidance systems, jet engines, and scientific instruments.

My interest in sharpness of rendering amounts almost to a fetish. The reason for it is my recognition of the superiority of the camera—eye in relation to my own eyes. Every sharp photograph shows me a multitude of details that would escape my notice in actuality, or shows subjects too small or remote to be otherwise clearly seen. As a result, every sharp photograph teaches me something new. The cumulative effect of having seen and studied thousands of such photographs has been a considerable gain in knowledge and insight. Although I realize that a softer form of rendition may have greater appeal to more imaginative and artistically inclined observers, a factual, sharp photograph is normally the most satisfying to my own curious, scientific mind.

### 6. The Life photographer Carl Mydans

This critically sharp portrait of a famous photojournalist at work shows the man as he really is, not falsified and diminished by the retoucher's airbrush or etching knife. To me, this is the only honest approach to portraiture, the only kind of rendition that does the subject justice and enables the observer of the photograph to form a valid impression.

### 7. Decaying oak leaf

To best preserve the fine detail of the venation and to produce the utmost in sharpness of rendition, I placed this decaying leaf in the enlarger as one would a negative, and printed it. By eliminating the negative, I simultaneously eliminated two common causes of decreased sharpness—film grain, and the slight loss of sharpness that results from optical reproduction, i. e., reduction of the image to the size of the film and subsequent enlargement of the negative on paper. I have successfully used this method of direct projection for the rendition of many thin objects of nature—leaves, feathers, fish scales, bits of sloughed-off snakeskin, transparent insect wings, and other subjects that demand extremely sharp rendition—when a graphic, silhouette-like quality is acceptable.

### 8. A look into the tube of a 16-inch navy gun
### 9. Close-up of a sea snail

As I have stressed, one of the fascinations of being a photographer is using the camera as a means to show things normally inaccessible or unnoticed, things that, because of their importance or beauty, are of interest. Here, the camera reveals the beauty of two functional forms—two helices—one produced by man to stabilize the trajectory of a projectile, the other grown by a mollusk, a protective shelter for the snail. Except for a few specialists, who but a photographer on assignment has the chance to investigate the inside of a big naval gun; and except for a few scientists, who but a photographer would pick up a little snail to record its form?

*10/11. A view of San Francisco*

In actuality, almost all the detail in this view would go unnoticed and only an impression of many little houses would remain. But when the same view is rendered with minute precision in photographic form, the eye can look long at streets and individual buildings, observing details that would take weeks to notice in reality.
I took this view with a 4 × 5-inch camera and a Zeiss Tele-Tessar of 40-cm focal length, using a Wrattan-A filter to minimize the effect of haze.

I have usually found that, with the exception of photographing people, photographing relatively large and relatively small subjects is more rewarding than photographing those that, precisely because of their size, present no problem in seeing. When these problem-less subjects are photographed, the resulting pictures often merely repeat what was already familiar to the eye and add nothing new to the experience of the observer.
To illustrate this, here are two close-ups from nature—a spiderweb, incomparably beautiful, exquisitely traced in liquid pearls of dew; and the track left by an insect that scrambled down the sandy slope of a dune. To my restless mind, each in its own way has cosmic implications, relates me to the Universe.

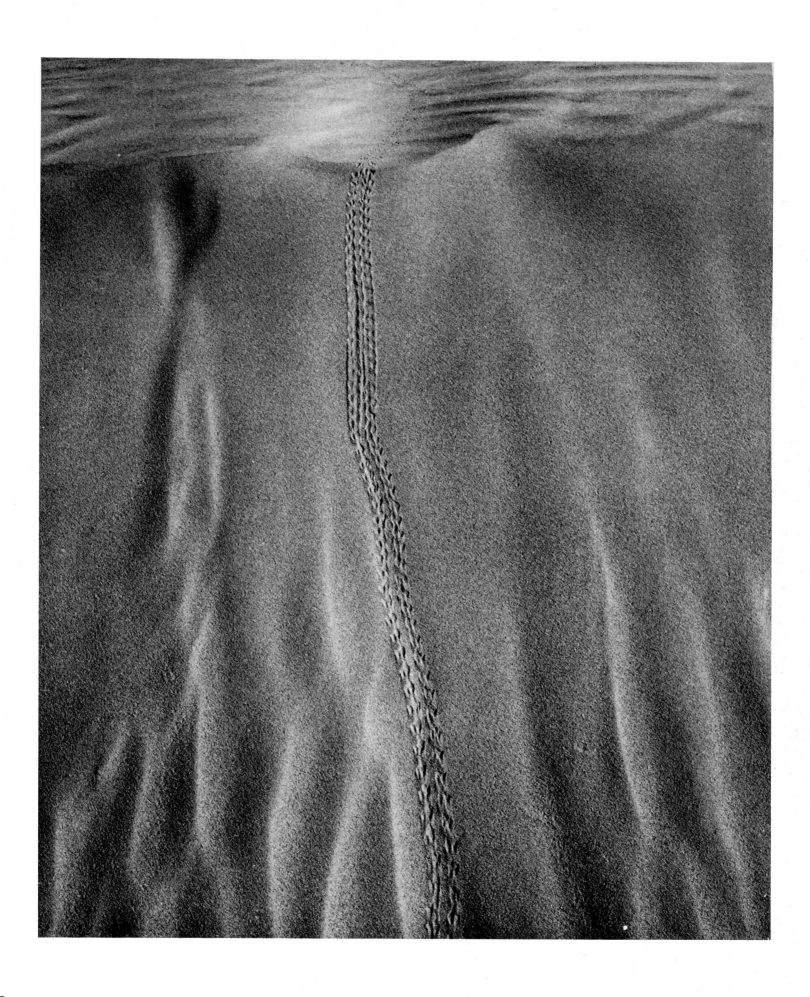

# III

## Graphic Black and White

Scientists tell us that dogs and many other animals cannot perceive color but see the world in different shades of gray. That people cannot see the world in such a way except through photography makes the black-and-white medium interesting in itself, and moreover, through it, things are seen anew and with different interest.

Color in photography, I believe, frequently falsifies a subject or makes it appear less attractive, as it often does in postcard or calendar views. Color also is often distasteful in portraits because of its inaccuracy: skin tones tinted with purple, green, or blue appear less natural than portraits in black and white. In many cases, color is superfluous because it contributes nothing to the characterization of the subject.

When color is not essential and a subject is taken in black and white, I feel that to make the most of its potentialities the translation of color into shades of gray should usually not be left to chance. I work to control both the contrast gradient and tone values of my pictures in order to produce the strongest possible graphic effects. This, as a rule, means strengthening the contrast, sometimes to the exclusion of all intermediate shades of gray, so that the entire rendition consists of areas of pure black and white.

Of course, I am well aware that according to aca-demic standards a photograph is considered at its best when it contains the greatest possible number of shades of gray, and that areas of pure black and white are frowned upon as "faults." But in my opinion, since a black-and-white photograph is by its very nature "unnatural," it matters little, from the aspect of subject recognition, whether the gray tone values correspond to those of the respective color shades. However, from a graphic point of view—pattern, composition, and design—it may matter enormously whether a specific shade is a lighter or darker gray, black, or white. The choice may make the difference between a weak, insipid rendition and one that effectively expresses the essence of a subject.

### 14. The physician

In this photograph, I tried to convey the essence of the concept "physician." The photograph is, as such, not a portrait but an abstraction, not an image of an individual but a synthesis of what I consider the essential attributes of a good physician: insight and objectivity, symbolized here through the traditional head mirror, which, like the bull's eye of a target, holds the patient's eye with almost hypnotic power. This, I felt, could be achieved only through the strongest available graphic means—pure black and white.

### 15. Mission church near Taos, New Mexico

Strong tonal contrast suggests power; lack of contrast, weakness. To symbolize in picture form the spiritual power of the Church, I used a red filter, paper of hard gradation, and extended exposure of the print, to transform the weak colors of the actual subject into suggestive, powerful black and white.

### 16. Sugar maples in winter
### 17. White oak in winter

Any student of trees knows that each species has its own characteristics. These, of course, extend

27

14

also to its "skeleton"—trunk and branches—whose development and organization make most trees as easily identifiable in winter without leaves as in summer when they bear leaves, flowers, or fruit.

These two pictures might be called graphs of trees. I deliberately eliminated, through backlight and silhouette, all intermediate shades of gray, to show each tree's growth characteristics in the cleanest and most expressive form.

*18. A geyser in Yellowstone Park*
*19. Bessemer converters blowing at night*

My favorite light is backlight. Whenever it can suitably be used, I consider it more effective than any other illumination, primarily because it creates stronger contrast of light and dark. Here, I used it to express in almost pure black and white the primeval power of the geyser and the roar of the Bessemers spewing their fire skyward.

*20. Dimout in New York, 1944*
*21. Grasses against a rainy sky*

If I have a choice, I prefer to use simple means of expression rather than complicated ones because, to me, simplicity of rendition produces feelings of strength and clarity, which are qualities desirable in any picture. These two photographs are examples of simplification carried to the point of abstraction. In both, I deliberately reduced the tone range to black and white. In the dimout shot, prolonged exposure would have brought out most of the details of the walls, and in the photograph of grasses, use of a filter would have brought out structural differentiation within the clouds. But rendition of such detail would not have fulfilled my purpose, which was to express feelings and mood, not to produce naturalistic studies: in the first, I wanted to record the somber mood of a wartime dimout; in the second, the feeling of relief from summer heat when the first moist breeze sways the grass as a prelude to rain.

15 ▶

# IV

*Semiabstract Photographs*

At a very early stage in my photographic career, I discovered that photography is not the simple "naturalistic medium of reproduction" it is popularly supposed to be; it is, on the contrary, a highly sophisticated, semiabstract form of visual representation. The ease with which its techniques can be mastered results in a belief that the making of *good, effective* photographs will also be easy. That it is not, is proved by the multitude of pictures that are dull and ineffective. The reason for the failure of many photographs lies in the fact that most of a subject's more important qualities, such as three-dimensionality, motion, life, or—in the case of black-and-white photographs—color, cannot be rendered directly but must be suggested through graphic symbols. Such symbols are used by all competent photographers. Space limitations make it impossible for me to discuss these here, and since I have discussed them elsewhere—the first time in my book *Fotografische Gestaltung,* and later and more extensively in *The Creative Photographer* and *Total Picture Control*—I refer the interested reader to those books.

Once one is convinced of the need for using symbols and has accepted the necessity of photographic control, he cannot resist finding out to what degree it is possible to influence the appearance of his pictures and to realize specific ideas in picture form. (Always, of course, by strictly photographic means and techniques, not by resorting to such interference as retouching or printing through special "screens.")

I began by investigating the possibilities of space control through the use of lenses of different focal length, and contrast control through the use of filters of different color and papers of different gradation. As I progressed, I found that graphic qualities—black-and-white distribution and contrast, composition, pattern, and design—are fully as important to the effect of a picture as other factors, such as angle of view, perspective, illumination, and scale. Actually, my experiments soon convinced me that graphic qualities are perhaps more important than other factors, since, in my opinion, a graphically interesting rendition of a nondescript subject as a rule produces a more striking picture than a photograph in which an interesting subject is poorly rendered. In the latter case, I look at the picture with a sense of frustration, knowing that, properly handled, the subject would have made a fascinating picture but the photographer has botched the job through his inability to see in photographic terms. Such examples are found particularly often in travel books and scientific reports in which highly interesting subjects are presented in pictures so dull one wants to weep.

Once I became thoroughly convinced of the importance of graphic qualities in a picture, I extended my search in that direction, and "discovered" the power of pure black and white, and with it the potentialities of negative prints. The next step was almost inevitable: I combined a negative and its diapositive (a positive contact print on film). I put these together in "sandwich form" but slightly off register, enlarged them, and produced a "bas-relief" print. By subsequently printing the "sandwich" on film I made a diapositive, which, when enlarged on paper, produced a negative bas-relief print in which the characteristic lines were white instead of black. A mistake in the darkroom (I turned on the white light while a print was still in the developer) resulted in my "discovering" the technique of solarization, which Man Ray in Paris, unknown to me, had found at just about the same time. And a mistake made by a friend of mine (he washed films in water that had become too warm) led to the process of controlled reticulation. If one wishes, these techniques can of course be used in different combinations. I wrote about my experience in finding and using them in my book *New Paths in Photography*.

Although the potentialities of the "graphic" techniques—bas-relief, solarization, and reticulation—are almost unlimited as far as the number of different forms of expression is concerned, the instances where they can be applied are obviously quite limited. I found these processes fascinating to experiment with, learned through their use a great deal about composition and design, and produced a number of photographs that appealed to me. Some of these are shown here. Eventually, however, I arrived at what then seemed to me a dead end, and I transferred my interests to other aspects of photography. But I have a feeling that I may take up these graphic techniques again at some time in the future.

## 22. Girl's head in darkness

The ultimate in simplification. Out of darkness—a vision, stirring the imagination to complete the lovely face.

## 23. Direct projection of a book scorpion

Four steps to greatest clarity. *Top left:* A cameraless direct projection of the "scorpion" on panchromatic film produced the solid, detail-less silhouette, shown here in twenty times linear magnification. *Top right:* A similar projection on infrared-sensitized film resulted in an improved, X-ray-like rendition showing the scorpion's internal structure. *Bottom left:* A diapositive made from the infrared negative produced a negative print which, white on black, further improved the clar-

ity of the image. *Bottom right:* By combining the infrared negative and diapositive to produce a bas-relief print an almost three-dimensional impression results, and creates the ultimate clarity of rendition.

## 24/25. Two negative prints

A new adventure in seeing. Transformation from the positive into the negative form, by reversing the familiar order of tone values, brings out many heretofore overlooked aspects of the subject and affords new insight. The substitution of light for dark and dark for light seems to invest objects with an inner light so that they appear to glow, and provides an entirely new visual experience.

## 26. Reticulation
## 27. Solarization

Symbolization of intangibles. These two photographs are, to my mind, graphic statements about feelings. In the one at the left, I tried to express the sensation of intense heat and the overpowering, shimmering light of high noon at the beach as I had experienced it; in the picture at the right, to preserve my impression of the beautiful silhouette of Södermalm, Stockholm, as I wished to remember it—freed from time-bound, unimportant detail.

## 28/29. Patterns of a leaf

Seven variations on a theme. I had fallen in love with the beautiful shape of a leaf. Wanting to render it in the most expressive form, I experimented with the graphic control processes. First I made a direct projection *(left-hand page, top, left)*, reversed it into the negative form *(top, center)*, then combined the two to make a bas-relief print *(top, right)*. From there, I went on to work with solarization *(bottom row)*, finally arriving at the print reproduced on the right-hand page, which, I feel, expresses the essence of the leaf's beauty.

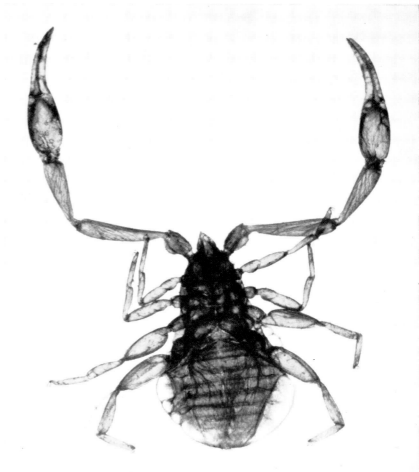
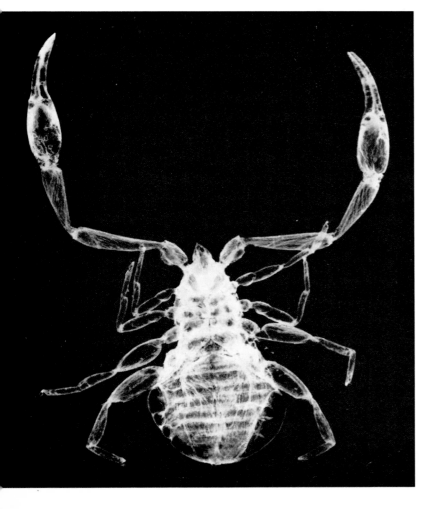
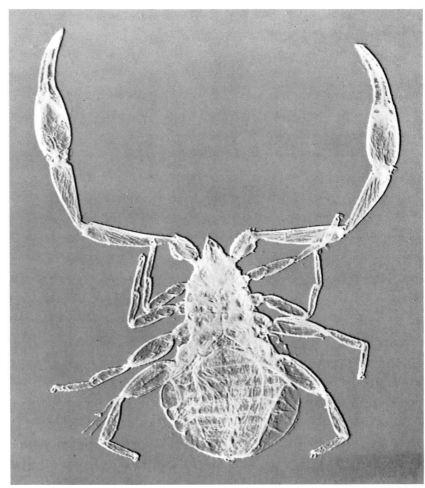

# V

*The Female Form*

There seems very little doubt woman is the oldest subject of the timeless compulsion that drives man to express concepts of importance in tangible form. It is not surprising that photographers, too, feel this same compulsion. Yet though they often try to express a concept through portrayal of the female form, they are usually unsuccessful. The main reason for their failure seems to lie in the fact that these images, although semiabstract insofar as they lack three-dimensionality, color, motion, and life, are nevertheless too realistic to represent a universal concept—the nude remaining a woman without clothes rather than becoming a figure that symbolizes womanhood.

I also have photographed the female nude, and in doing so, tried to apply to my photographs what I have learned from contemplating good sculpture of the female form. A good sculptor deliberately eliminates nonessential detail, de-personalizes the human form, and through simplification and abstraction brings out universal aspects. It is in this respect that most photographs of nudes fail—they are too anatomically correct, too detailed, too representative of one woman to take the mind of the observer beyond that particular form to those universal aspects of femininity that include such timeless concepts as beauty, love, fertility, motherhood, and the mysteries of birth and death.

When I photograph the nude I have to rely on techniques that are basically alien to my way of working: I deliberately offset, if not destroy, the ability of the lens to record minute detail with utmost precision. However, I achieve this, *not* by retouching the negatives or prints or otherwise subjecting them to alien techniques, but by using typically photographic means: strong light and deep shadows; outline and silhouette; and the "graphic" techniques of bas-relief, reticulation, and solarization.

Included in this section are a number of photographs of female nudes taken from my book *Maids, Madonnas, and Witches—Women in Sculpture from Prehistoric Times to Picasso.* In these photographs, my approach had to be quite different, since the essential work of abstraction had already been done by the sculptor. My task, as I saw it, was to bring out and to interpret, in terms of black and white, the artist's intent as embodied in the original.

This involved giving the most careful consideration to factors such as angle of view (a sculpture—a form in the round—presents an infinite number of different angles from which usually only one view can be chosen); illumination (the wrong type of light and the wrong type of shadows can falsify, even totally destroy, the effect of any sculpture); cropping (since a two-dimensional photograph and a three-dimensional sculpture are two completely different things, I believe that to achieve the strongest effect it is not only permissible, but often necessary, to limit the rendition to only part of the sculpture; in other words, to crop the image in the negative); and contrast control in the print (to amplify and complement the task of the illumination).

### 30. Standing nude

By deliberately reducing tonal values to three main shades—black, gray, and white—eliminating textural detail, and emphasizing line and form, I tried to give adequate expression to the universal aspects of this strong and beautiful figure.

## 31. Girl at the beach

This is admittedly a rather naturalistic photograph. But I feel that the sculptural quality of this young body makes its own clean and strong impression, to which I can add nothing.

## 32. Girl looking down at the water

A simple statement made in the simplest graphic terms. Dark planes of shadow set off by small accents of light convey the contemplative mood of this young woman.

## 33. Reticulated nude

This is an attempt to utilize the pointillistic effect of reticulation to de-personalize the rendition, unify the picture elements, and stylize this study to the degree necessary to convey universal aspects of Woman.

## 34/35. Two bas-relief prints

The broad, bold strokes of the bas-relief process permit a photographer to emphasize essential forms and simultaneously suppress unwanted textural detail. The effect will be the stronger, the simpler the form and tonal range of the subject.

## 36/37. Two solarized prints

In contrast to the boldness of bas-relief renditions, which is reminiscent of woodcuts, solarized prints suggest the elegance of engravings. Lines of often incredible delicacy form the boundaries of empty space, while interpenetration of positive and negative picture elements further strengthens the feeling of mystery and unreality.

## 38. Nude in black and white

In this study, I use massive black sparsely accentuated with white to de-personalize the figure, further strengthening the universal aspects by masking the face in shadow. Here the female form is stylized to the point of abstraction, the statement deliberately left incomplete. But enough is shown to stir the imagination and induce the observer to complete the image in his mind.

## 39. Wooden fetish of the Bambara tribe, Western Sudan

The suggestive power of this fertility idol is so strong in the object itself, it was apparent to me that the simpler my approach in photographing it, the greater my chance of transferring its force to the print—so I photographed the statue as a silhouette.

## 40. Detail of a bronze figurine by Gaston Lachaise
## 41. Aurignacian limestone figurine, ca. 30,000 B. C.

A marked similarity in concept and approach seems to relate these two figurines despite the interval of some 30,000 years that separates them. Although one is highly sophisticated and the other primitive and naive, both convey to an extraordinarily high degree the spirit of fertility—Woman as the giver of life. It was this feeling of richness and generosity, of fullness and abundance, that I wished to present in my photographs.

## 42. Indian bronze statue of Parwati (fifteenth century)
## 43. Egyptian limestone torso (4th dynasty, 2680—2560 B. C.)

Each age and culture has its own concept of feminine beauty. These two figures seem to me typical of their respective times and places of origin. To transfer their haunting beauty to film and paper, I relied mainly on carefully controlled illumination whose highlights and shadows preserve the subtle outlines and forms.

## 44/45. Torso, by Gaston Lachaise, Museum of Modern Art, New York

Sometimes a single photograph is insufficient to represent a three-dimensional form adequately. I felt this to be true in the case of Lachaise's magnificent sculpture. Front and three-quarter views are shown side by side because each complements the other to such a degree that one seemed incomplete without the other. Only in combination do they give an impression comparable to that of seeing the original in the round.

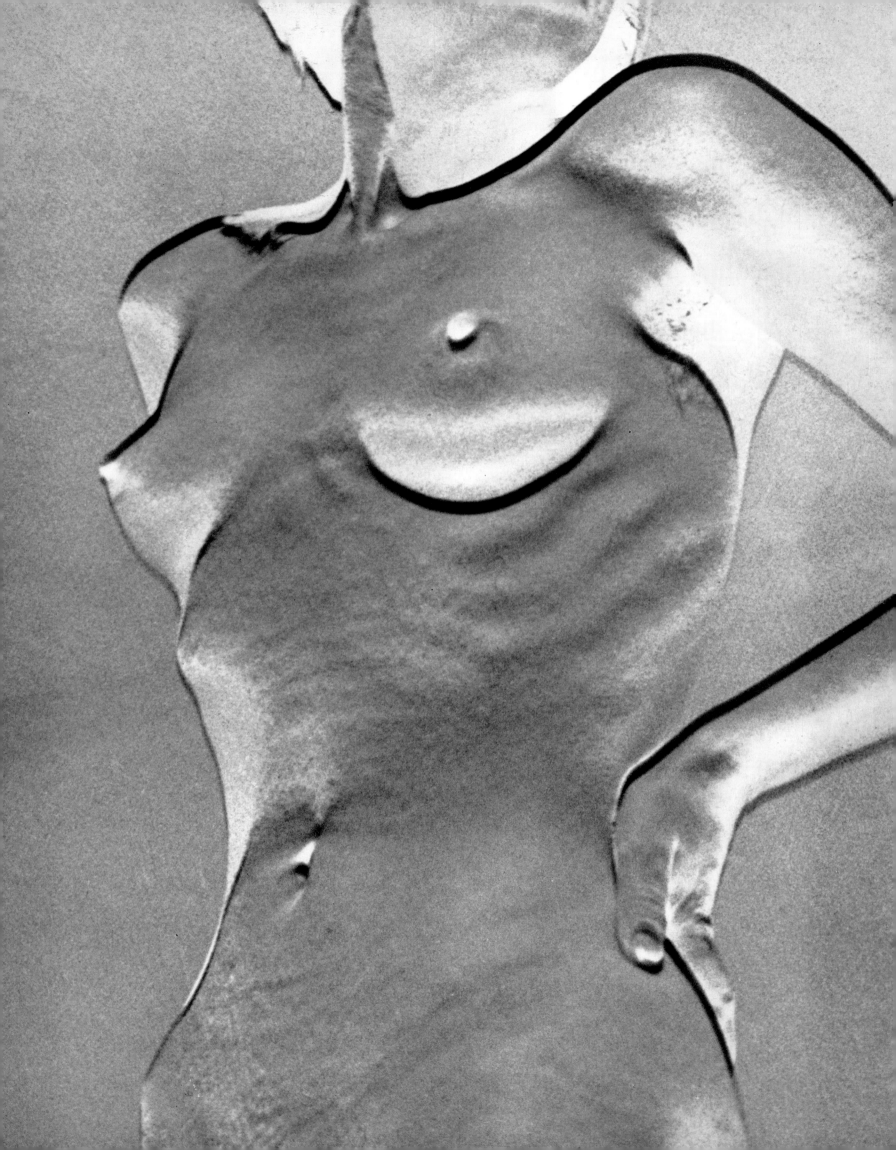

# VI

*The Undistorted Space*

The concept of perspective is inseparably linked to that of distortion. For example, the more abruptly actual parallel lines appear to converge in a photograph, the stronger the impression of depth—an effect well illustrated by many wide-angle photographs. Such convergence is of course a distortion of reality, since the lines were truly parallel. Similarly, the smaller that an object of known dimensions is rendered in a photograph in relation to another object, the greater the distance in depth between the two appears to be. But this illusion of depth—the result of diminution, another manifestation of perspective—is likewise based upon distortion. It occurs even if the object rendered as the smaller of the two is in reality much larger than the object that appears large in the photograph. For instance, a distant building or mountain would appear much smaller in a photograph than a person close to the camera, and in this reversal of size, reality is rendered "distorted."

Normally, we accept a certain degree of distortion—convergence and diminution—in photographs, but in some we object to it. Although the laws of perspective apply in the vertical plane as well as in the horizontal or any other plane, in photographs of buildings, for example, the upward convergence of vertical lines—lines that are actually parallel—is usually felt to be a distortion of reality and rejected as a fault. For this reason, in photographs of buildings, interiors, furniture, and many closeups of objects with parallel sides, we render verticals parallel to avoid the feeling of distortion, even though this involves "correcting" perspective by using the swings and tilts of a view camera.

Obviously, a conflict exists between two different, mutually exclusive objectives: if one wishes to create an illusion of depth in one's pictures, distortion must be used; but if one wishes the impressions he creates to conform as closely as possible to reality, then distortion must be suppressed.

I have been conscious of the conflict between distortion and depth on one side, and freedom from distortion and lack of depth on the other, ever since I became seriously interested in photography, and have given it much thought. I see this conflict as a choice: which is more important, the illusion of depth or the suppression of distortion? I prefer to avoid distortion—partly because I consider distortion a falsification, therefore something to be avoided; and partly because the illusion of depth in a photograph is not entirely dependent upon perspective and distortion but can be created through juxtaposition of dark foreground and light background or contrast between sharpness and unsharpness (selective focus), two means that do not involve distortion. Besides, complete elimination of distortion is not possible; hence, controlling it does not mean that one's photographs will be entirely devoid of the depth that it creates.

As any photographer knows, the shorter the relative focal length of the lens and the shorter the distance between subject and camera, the more pronounced the effects of perspective and diminution—i. e., of distortion—and vice versa. I have made use of this fact from the time that I took my first telephotographs in 1936 in Stockholm, by working as far as practicable with a lens of the longest focal length and photographing my subjects from the greatest distance that circumstances would permit, to keep my renditions as free from distortion as possible. The resulting tele-perspective is characterized by two qualities: in relation to one another, the true proportions of objects are largely preserved—i. e., small objects appear relatively small in the picture even when they were comparatively close to the camera, and large objects appear relatively large and dominant even when they were far away from the camera; and space appears strangely compressed. However, the apparent compression of space is only an optical illusion. This fact can be verified by making the following experiment: From an identical camera position, take two photographs of the same distant subject, one with a lens of standard focal length, the other with a telephoto lens. If you enlarge the negative taken with the lens of standard focal length *to the same scale* as the negative taken with the telephoto lens is enlarged (which, of course, involves a different degree of magnification), you will find that as far as perspective is concerned, the section from the standard negative corresponding to the area covered by the tele-negative will be identical to the tele-negative except in sharpness. If one print is superimposed upon the other they will be seen to register perfectly, thus proving their perspectives identical.

I find this typical telephoto perspective extraordinarily beautiful. Photographs containing it give a feeling of monumentality not found in any other type of rendition. Somehow, they seem more true than ordinary photographs, and that after all is not surprising, for they are closer to reality. The telephotographs shown here will confirm this fact.

### 46. Three telephoto cameras

*Top, left:* This is the homemade camera described in the introductory text. The strong rubber band connecting the camera back and the tripod was applied to dampen vibrations.

*Top, right:* Here is an Exacta 6 × 6 cm, equipped with a Zeiss Magnar variable telephoto lens of 45-plus cm focal length. I used it to make the picture on pages 48/49. Note how the lens is braced—the first version of my "pentapod."

*Bottom:* This is my oldest homemade 40-inch telephoto camera, 4 × 5 inches, mounted on the second version of my "pentapod." The crosspiece connected by guy wires to the front legs of the pentapod is a wind brace. I used this camera to make the photographs on pages 52 to 57 and 62 and 63.

### 47. Approach to New York from the west

Suggesting tombstones left by a race of giants, the skyscrapers of midtown Manhattan rise in ghostly pallor from behind the ridge that borders the Hudson on the New Jersey side. Only from a great distance, through the use of an extreme telephoto lens, can these towers be made to appear in all their enormous size. To the eye, they are mere specks on the horizon.

### 48/49. The skyline of midtown Manhattan

The small town in the foreground is approximately two miles from the camera; the distant skyline, fourteen. Yet in spite of the great difference in distance, because diminution is held to a minimum, the houses in the foreground appear relatively small, whereas the faraway skyscrapers appear huge, still dominating the scene as befits their tremendous size.

### 50/51. Fifth Avenue, New York

Two versions of the same street—at noon in July, and during a blizzard in March. Both show New York at its worst.

### 52/53. Downtown Manhattan

Only a telephoto lens with its relatively true perspective can convey the full grimness and the inhuman aspects of this part of New York.

### 54. Downtown Manhattan, New York
### 55. George Washington Bridge, New York

I made these photographs with a 40-inch Dallmeyer Grandac telephoto lens on 4 × 5-inch film.

In both, the true proportions of all the picture elements are almost completely preserved, and it is this that creates the feeling of monumentality.

## 56/57. Midtown Manhattan, North River waterfront

This photograph seems to me to give particularly convincing proof of the desirability of "distortion-free" rendition: small boats in the foreground appear small in the picture, large buildings in the background appear large, as they are in actuality. Had this view been taken, as such views usually are, from a shorter distance with a lens of standard focal length, the small boats would have been rendered disproportionately large and the large buildings disproportionately small—perspective and diminution would have combined to produce a thoroughly distorted image of reality.

## 58. New York, West 20th Street
## 59. Television aerial, Empire State Building

A housewife hanging up laundry in a desert of brick and cement; two maintenance men precariously clinging to spidery steel. Only a super telephoto lens could have given me the kind of un-distorted picture I had in mind—the true proportions showing man dominated and dwarfed by a world he himself has created.

## 60/61. Oil derricks, Signal Hill, California

In a man-made forest, giants of wood and steel ceaselessly and tirelessly, day and night, suck oil from the ground, their taproots probing thousands of feet into the earth. I made this picture with a 40-cm Zeiss Tele-Tessar on $4 \times 5$-inch film, deliberately to "compress" space and thus convey the claustrophobic feeling of being caught in a monstrous maze that I experienced that summer day when I photographed Signal Hill.

## 62/63. Mt. Shasta, California

Towering more than 14,000 feet above sea level, an extinct volcano thrusts its icy crags toward the sky. The closer one approaches it, the more one loses sight of the mountain itself, and to photograph it as seen here I had to be some ninety miles away. At that distance, of course, a super telephoto lens had to be used to give sufficiently large scale.

# VII

*The Near and the Small*

Some of the pleasantest and most exciting hours I have spent in photographing have been devoted to making close-ups. I never tire of studying small, interesting objects, getting closer and closer to them as I rack out the lens, watching their images grow on the groundglass and their blurred forms become sharp, and experiencing that indescribable fascination of seeing hitherto unseen wonders take shape before my eyes.

In addition to being an inexhaustible source of intellectual and aesthetic experience, close-up photography has a strictly practical attraction: it can be engaged in anywhere at any time with very little expenditure for equipment. All one needs is a lens of short focal length, a camera that has a groundglass and an extension bellows or tubes, a tripod, and a couple of photoflood lamps or speedlights. Subjects in endless variety can be found everywhere. Some of my favorite pictures are of things discovered in my own home or garden, like the frost pattern formed on a windowpane (page 67) or a spiderweb (page 72). I rarely take a walk without carrying a few glass vials or other little containers to hold small objects of nature that I may find and wish to study more closely with my camera. If one walks in the woods or fields or along the seashore, there are many things to be found—shells and snails, skeletons of fish, feath-ers, insects, spiders, caterpillars, seed pods or interesting seeds, crystals, and other natural forms—and the search for such things not only makes one look more intently at his surroundings but often pays rich dividends in the unexpected discovery of strange and beautiful objects.

Although I prefer to photograph whatever I find in its natural surroundings, this is not always possible. In such cases, I take my finds home and there try to duplicate their original setting. This usually is not too difficult, since the area that needs to be reconstructed for photographic purposes rarely exceeds half a square foot. I put live insects and caterpillars on their own food plants or leaves before photographing them, and often keep them for days and weeks to record their life cycles before I give them their freedom. I once spent the better part of a summer in this pleasant sort of work, doing a picture essay on insects for *Life;* thirty-two color photographs from this set were subsequently reproduced in *Living Insects of the World.*

Speaking of color photographs, I believe that renditions in color and in black and white are equally valid; neither is superior, and the choice between the two should, in my opinion, always be made in relation to the specific demands of the subject itself. Each medium offers certain advantages, each has certain limitations. A rendition in color is more naturalistic but more difficult to control than a rendition in black and white, which is more abstract and therefore more subject to control. Thus, in black and white, the photographer has more leeway to create specific impressions. Whenever the decision is left to me, I use color only if color is one of the outstanding qualities of the subject; unless color contributes decisively to its characterization, I prefer to work in black and white. I mention this consideration now because this is the first chapter in which color photographs are shown; here, as in subsequent chapters in this book in which color photographs appear, color was always a necessary picture element, a factor without which a particular photograph would have been less meaningful.

## 64. Rear view of a trapdoor spider

Magnified approximately twenty times linear here, this subject provides an example of the fascinating discoveries one makes when working in the field of close-up photography. Who would imagine that this little spider has on its rear end a pattern that looks like a replica of an Inca sun symbol?

## 65. Some technical aspects of close-up photography

*Top, left:* The author photographing a live insect with a Hasselblad equipped with a bellows of his own design and a synchronized speedlight. For quick, accurate focusing at any predetermined scale of magnification, the entire camera slides back and forth on an auxiliary track, which is independent of its rack-and-pinion focusing drive. A preset, semiautomatic, homemade device based upon a rotating ring and a pin permits me to focus with the lens wide open and, at the instant before the exposure, to stop down the diaphragm to a preset aperture without looking away from the subject or groundglass.
*Top, right:* This picture shows how simple a close-up setup can be. The subject—the tooth-studded jawbone of a skate—is held in place by a C-clamp fastened to a small cardboard box weighted down by a stone.
A gray cardboard provides a neutral background. An ordinary desk lamp and a small spotlight provide the illumination. The camera is a $3^1/_4 \times 4^1/_4$-inch Linhof Technika with fully drawn triple bellows extension.
*Bottom:* A close-up of the teeth of a skate magnified approximately twenty-five times linear. This is the photograph made with the setup shown in the picture above.

## 66. A section from a 900-year-old Inca feather hat

Magnified approximately three times natural size, this close-up shows details and texture normally not seen by the unaided eye. Selection of the most important area of the hat accentuates the bold

design. If rendered in black and white, the subject would have lost its most important feature, for color is an essential part of the design.

## 67. Frost pattern on a windowpane

Another discovery made through close-up photography was the amazing similarity in organization and growth between minute ice patterns (here shown magnified approximately twenty times linear) and the feathers of a bird or the leaves of certain plants. One wonders whether this similarity is mere coincidence, or the manifestation of the universality of certain laws governing growth and organization in nature. Or whether it suggests a deeper relationship between all the elements of the world, inanimate and animate.

## 68. Camellia blossom
## 69. Rectifier tubes

Strong, glowing color transforms common objects into magical things—a fallen blossom floats on dark swamp waters like a symbol of purity rising above iridescent corruption; and deep in the interior of an electronic computer, rectifiers, like unearthly flowers, shine with mysterious blue light.

## 70. Detail of the rim of a seashell
## 71. Caterpillar of the spicebush swallowtail

This is what I love: to track down hidden beauty and to discover the underlying, structural design—the rim, suggesting a breaking wave crested with foam, which strengthens a mollusk's shell; the caterpillar that looks with eyes that are not eyes but only eyelike spots of color, perhaps given to it by nature to frighten off its enemies. . . .

## 72. Web of the yellow garden spider
## 73. Growth pattern of a weed

The contemplation of nature provides material for endless speculation: How did the spider learn to spin its web? What makes a plant's growth symmetrical, radiating starlike in all directions, each leaf repeating the same design? Although photographing a marvel does not solve its riddle, it leads to thought about it and aesthetic enjoyment of it, and perhaps to respect and reverence for all natural things and the realization that all are one.

74. *Yellow swallowtail on a raspberry flower*
75. *Detail of a reed stalk*
76/77. *Eyes of two species of deer flies*
78. *Nest of the paper wasp*
79. *Praying mantis eating a grasshopper*

Any photographer who has an inquiring mind and open eyes will find close-up photography an endlessly rewarding field, particularly if he chooses subjects in which he has a genuine interest. My favorites are insects. In the course of catching and photographing them I have learned many things that may be of use to others. The main qualification is patience—something I wish I had more of—closely followed by a persistence that borders on mulishness. If something doesn't work the first time, try again and again; perhaps it *will* work the tenth time. Catching insects is easier than finding them—many are marvelously camouflaged. A good way to collect some full-grown insects as well as those at various stages of development is to hold a light-colored umbrella upside-down beneath branches or shrubs and rap these sharply with a heavy stick. The blows will dislodge a good many insects that are too well hidden to be found otherwise. Many winged insects take off at the slightest sign of danger, making it almost impossible for a person to get within shooting range. I catch such insects in a butterfly net and photograph them indoors *at night* in carefully prepared settings that duplicate their natural surroundings. It is a surprising fact that most daylight insects are inactive at night *even in a reasonably well illuminated room* and will not fly away from a focusing light. Night-flying insects, inactive by day,

present no problem to a photographer. I dislike the often-recommended practice of making lively insects tractable by chilling them in a refrigerator. Insects so treated are too numb to behave naturally. By the time they are sufficiently warmed to appear natural, they are also sufficiently warmed for a quick takeoff and thus frustrate the efforts of the chiller. Instead of chilling them, I put them in a wire cage and entice them with food—flowers, if necessary sprinkled with a few drops of sugar water, for butterflies and bumblebees; half-spoiled fruit for hornets and wasps; live grasshoppers for mantises, etc. I cut a hole in the wire screen of the cage, poke the lens through it, prefocus on the food, and wait. Usually I don't have to wait long before I get my picture. For close-ups of this kind I prefer to work with a small ring-light strobe lamp that encircles the lens and produces a shadowless illumination. This strobe lamp is particulary desirable in photographing subjects in color at very close range, where it is difficult—if not impossible—to illuminate the subject adequately with side-or toplight because the lens gets in the way, casting a shadow where one wants it least. To make the photographs of deer-fly eyes on pages 76 and 77, I used a trick that the greatest of all close-up photographers, Dr. Roman Vishniac, taught me: I stuck a wire through a leaf and fastened the live insect to it by joining the tip of the insect's abdomen to the tip of the wire with a drop of quickdrying glue. The insect doesn't seem to mind this, for it rests easily and naturally on the leaf without attempting flight, making it possible to get as close as one wishes with the lens. The wire itself is hidden and does not show in the photograph. To simplify focusing and exposure (which, of course, must be increased beyond normal, depending on the degree of image magnification), I prefocus my lens in accordance with a predetermined scale of rendition and lock it in position, then do the actual focusing by moving the entire camera back and forth until the image appears sharp.

# VIII

*Professional People*

Man, unlike any other species, has been able to survive a variety of external conditions, to reverse the specialization that places limits upon other living things and to conquer, through his intellect, environments from which he was originally barred. Wingless, he flies; armored, he can live beneath the sea; protected by many ingenious devices, he can go unhampered into environments inaccessible to any other form of life or limited to specific species. Though all men, except for racial and individual differences, are in appearance very much alike, each one is superficially transformed by the trappings of his particular profession, so that a man in a diver's suit and helmet, for example, seems divested of human attributes. Encased in, or appendaged with, the instruments of his work, he often takes on totally different appearances that, in their variety, are somewhat akin to the differences that exist in the highly specialized forms found throughout nature. And when thus superficially transformed, he sometimes looks stranger than the strangest of beasts.

In my work for *Life* I have photographed specialists in many professions. Equipped with the devices necessary to their work, they were changed into beings who looked unreal and sometimes monstrous, appealing to the imagination like creatures from another world entirely. As a photographer, I found them fascinating, and from those that I photographed I here include sixteen.

These are not studies of hired models masquerading as, for instance, a photographer, a diamond cutter, or a doctor, but people photographed in relation to their work, appearing fantastic because the equipment necessary to their work creates this impression.

To convey as far as possible what is typical to each profession portrayed, I have, of course, deliberately dramatized each in rendition, primarily through the use of light and by close cropping. Through this approach I sought to preserve the immediacy of my impressions and convey to the observer something of the excitement and intensity that surrounds these people when they are absorbed in their work.

## 80. *The photo-journalist*

The epitome of intensified seeing. Directed by eye and brain, with split-second accuracy the precision machine records and preserves the fleeting event.

## 81. *The diamond cutter*

Deliberation, knowledge, and experience. Personification of the patience demanded by the weeks and months of study that often precede the moment of cleaving a priceless stone—with a fortune involved in the decision.

## 82. *The physician*

The thoughtful, serious face of a man who knows of human suffering, and is deeply aware of his responsibility—and his power.

## 83. *The fencer*

*En garde*—statuesque outward calm at the instant of highest tension, just before the duel starts.

## 84. *The physicist*

The gaze of an idealist, a seer: expressive of a

mind dedicated to the slow and wearisome search for truth.

### 85. The sculptor

Strong, sensitive, expressive hands delicately shape the wax under the guidance of the artist's eye.

### 86. The research scientist

After months or years of work, frustration, and hope—the moment of truth.

### 87. The laboratory technician

With delicate, tender touch, a young woman candles an egg to check the development of an implanted growth.

### 88. The spectroscopist

A "miracle" of science. The deviation of light passing through a diffraction grating mosaic, which is one of the most powerful research tools of astronomy, here causes the apparent shift of the head from the body.

### 89. The arachnologist

Even lower forms of life, like this whip scorpion, are worth attention, for studying them can contribute to our understanding of the world.

### 90. An industrial worker

Not a man-eating monster, but a man protected by a gas mask so that he can work in a poisonous atmosphere. Is this perhaps the face of things to come?

### 91. The football player

The grotesque effect is produced by the curving bar of Lucite that protects the wearer's face.

### 92. The welder

A robot breathing sparks of fire? No, a welder at work in a shipyard.

### 93. The deep-sea diver

Looking like a monster dredged from the deep—or a mine adrift at night—this sphere of brass and glass is the protective headgear of a navy diver ready to descend.

### 94. The skindiver

What at first looks like an old-fashioned carriage lantern or the headlight of a locomotive is—as the blonde hair reveals—a young woman in a skindiver's faceplate.

### 95. The coxswain

A human megaphone, a slave driver, exhorting his crew to make the ultimate effort for victory.

80-95. These photographs were made with a Rolleiflex, Kodak Tri-X film, and were developed in Kodak Developer D-76.

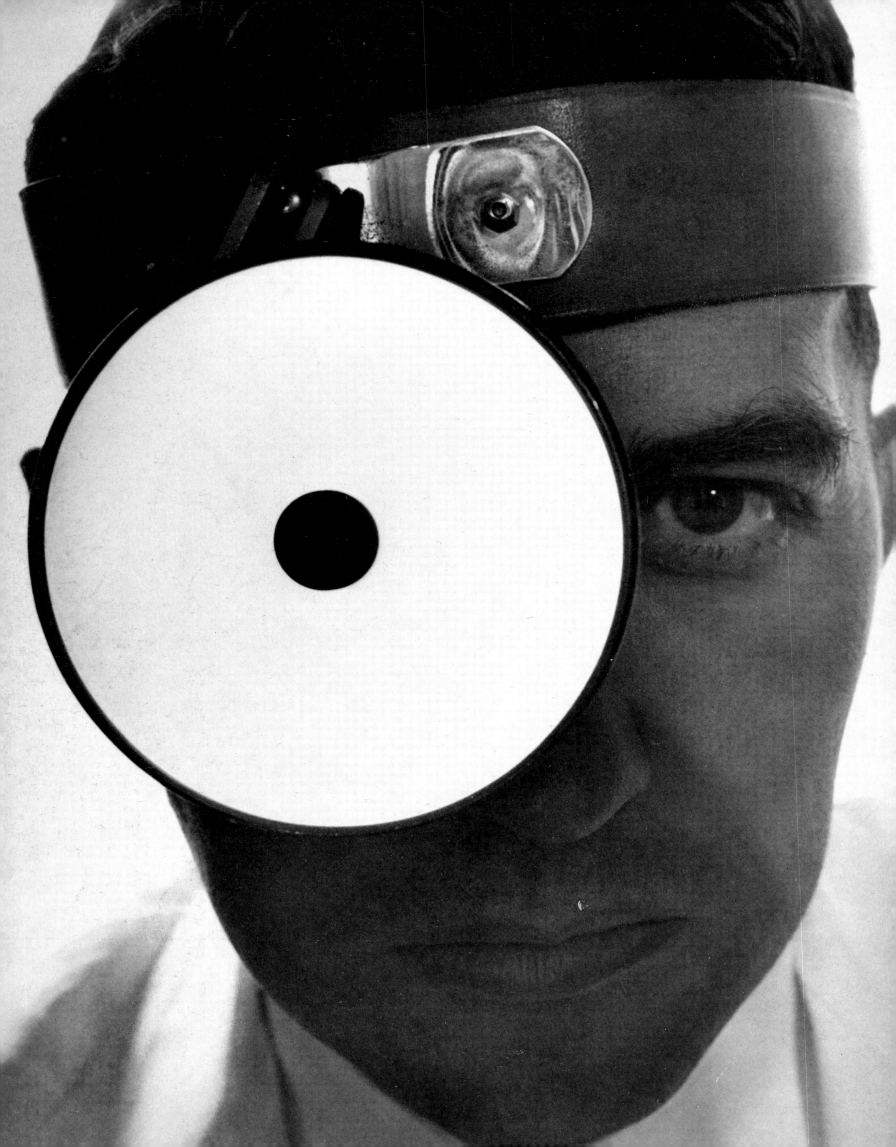

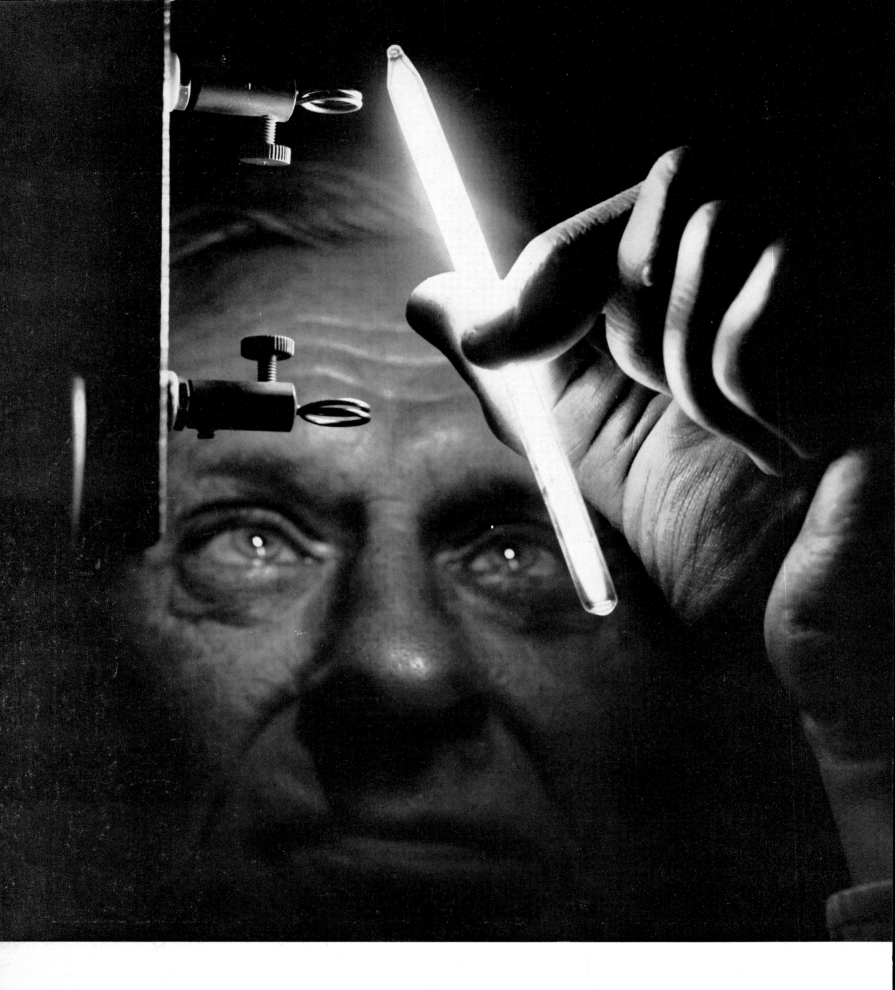

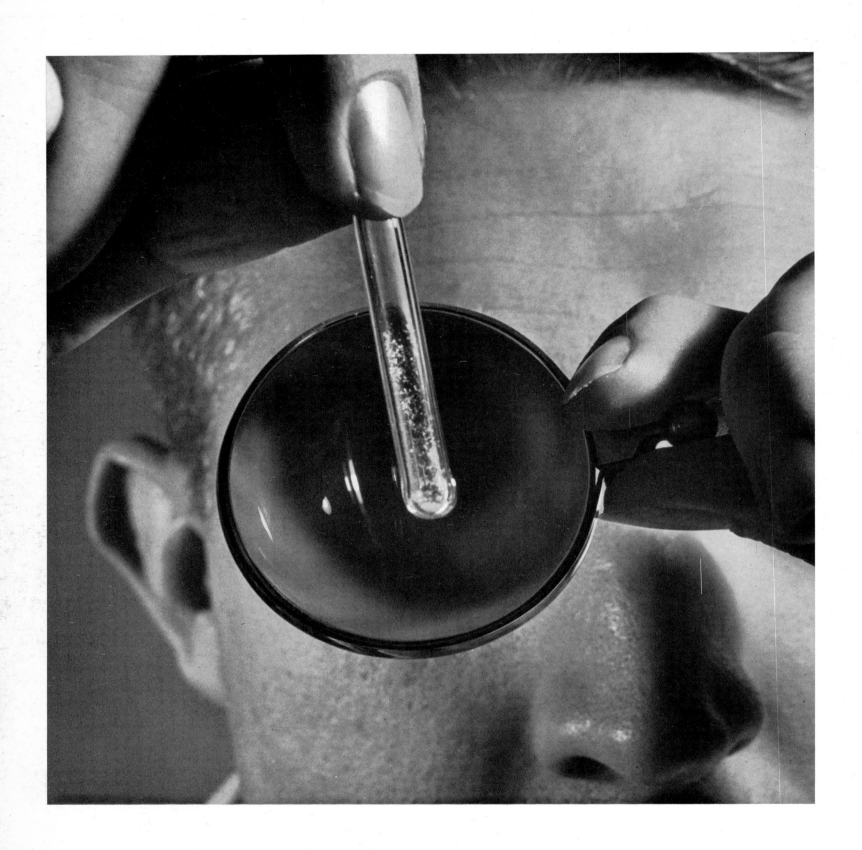

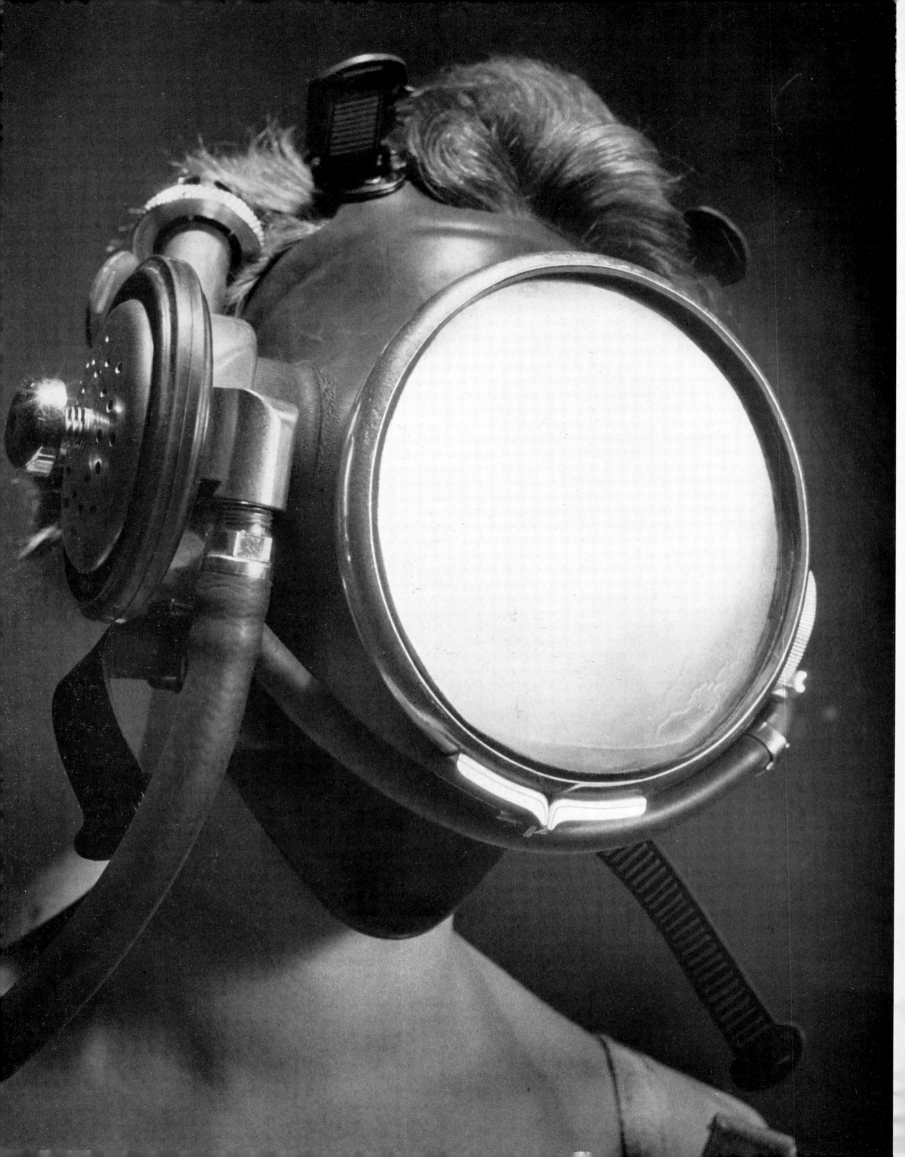

# IX

*Motion and Light*

It seems to me that nowhere in photography is there a greater need for the use of symbols than in the case of pictures in which concepts of motion and light are to be expressed. Motion is inseparably linked to space and time, two concepts that cannot be rendered directly in a photograph. Many photographs of racing cars published in motor magazines, for instance, express no sensation of speed, though it could have been produced in symbolic form. Instead, the cars appear to be at a standstill. And the concept of light—direct light—is inseparable from the concepts of radiance and luminosity. If these qualities are to be suggested in a photograph, symbols must be employed.

Fortunately, a number of symbols can be effectively used to suggest these concepts. Motion, for example, can be expressed in graphic form by means of blur, time exposure, panning, multiple exposure and printing, picture sequences, and composition. And the radiance of direct light can be symbolized through flare and halation, star patterns, diffusion, and out-of-focus rendition. Space limitations here make it impossible to elaborate upon these interesting techniques, but I have fully discussed and illustrated them in my book *Total Picture Control*.

The following photographs are the result of ex-periments I made in the symbolization of motion and light. Experimenting is necessary because most of these symbols must be used with precision; even a slight degree of change greatly influences the effect. For example, to express a certain degree of speed, a specific amount of blur is needed: if the blur is too little, the motion appears too slow; conversely, if the blur is too great, the motion appears too fast or the moving subject becomes unrecognizable. Similarly, in the symbolization of light, too little halation may fail to produce the desired effect of radiance, whereas too much would destroy the picture.

## 96. Morning in the forest

Sunlight striking the lens reinforces the starlike design that radial shafts of light cut into the early morning mist, and re-creates the sensation of direct radiant light.

## 97. Bulldozers working on a coal pile

The contrast between the sharply rendered ground and the deliberately blurred mound of coal that tumbles before the bulldozer produces the illusion of motion.

## 98. Speed on the open road
## 99. Exploding phosphor bomb

Time exposure and centripetal forces produced the similarity in design in these two photographs, in which motion is expressed through carefully controlled blur.

*Left:* An attempt to express in graphic form the exhilarating feeling of driving a fast car over a tree-lined country road.

*Right:* The frightful spectacle of an exploding phosphor bomb showering its surroundings with liquid fire.

*100/101. Amusement park at night*

These stunning designs of motion and light, though invisible to the eye, existed in latent form and were recorded by the camera in their precise geometrical beauty.

*102/103. Night in the city*

Artists have long used a star design to suggest radiance. Photographers can produce the same symbol by placing a wire screen in front of the lens. In this case I used two crossed wire screens to express, by means of eightpointed stars, the glitter of lights in the city at night.

*104/105. Brooklyn Bridge, New York*

In this shot, halation combined with time exposure—which recorded the motion of river traffic in lines of light—conveys the festive and magic impression of a luminous metropolis at night.

*106/107. Two views of Hamburg before the war*

I took these pictures because the light expressed the feeling of these city views. Had the light been different, I probably would not have photographed either.
*At the left,* sun-diffused mist, in making the air tangible, intensified the feeling of space.
*At the right,* the halos that encircled the street lamps in the fog brought to mind the halos of saints, and seemed in that association to belong with the facade of the Baroque church looming in the darkness.

*108/109. Four views of a mobile*

This mobile is an artist's version of the solar system: the sun circled by the earth, which in turn is circled by the moon, with the Big Dipper above. It was designed to be seen in motion. I made one record shot, a static view, to orient the observer *(top left)*. It, of course, is inadequate for anything more than that because in it the mobile appears uninteresting, whereas actually it is quite striking when its components slowly revolve. To capture the feeling of circling cosmic bodies I made some twenty different time exposures, three of which are shown here. By using different techniques—photoflood illumination, repeating stroboscopic light, continuous and interrupted exposures—I made some strange and astonishing graphs, which, I think, not only are beautiful but also seem to suggest in symbolic form the slow, revolving paths of celestial spheres.

*110/111. Tracks of the stars*

To me, photographs of star tracks are most thought-provoking, for they are a reminder of the universe, of infinity, eternity, and the unity of man and stars.
The photograph at the left shows the Statue of Liberty in New York Harbor, holding high the torch of freedom in the star-studded night. At the right is a photograph of the big radio telescope at Greenbank, West Virginia, taken as it tracked a star.

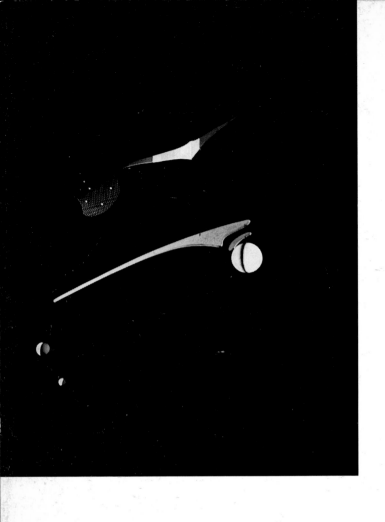

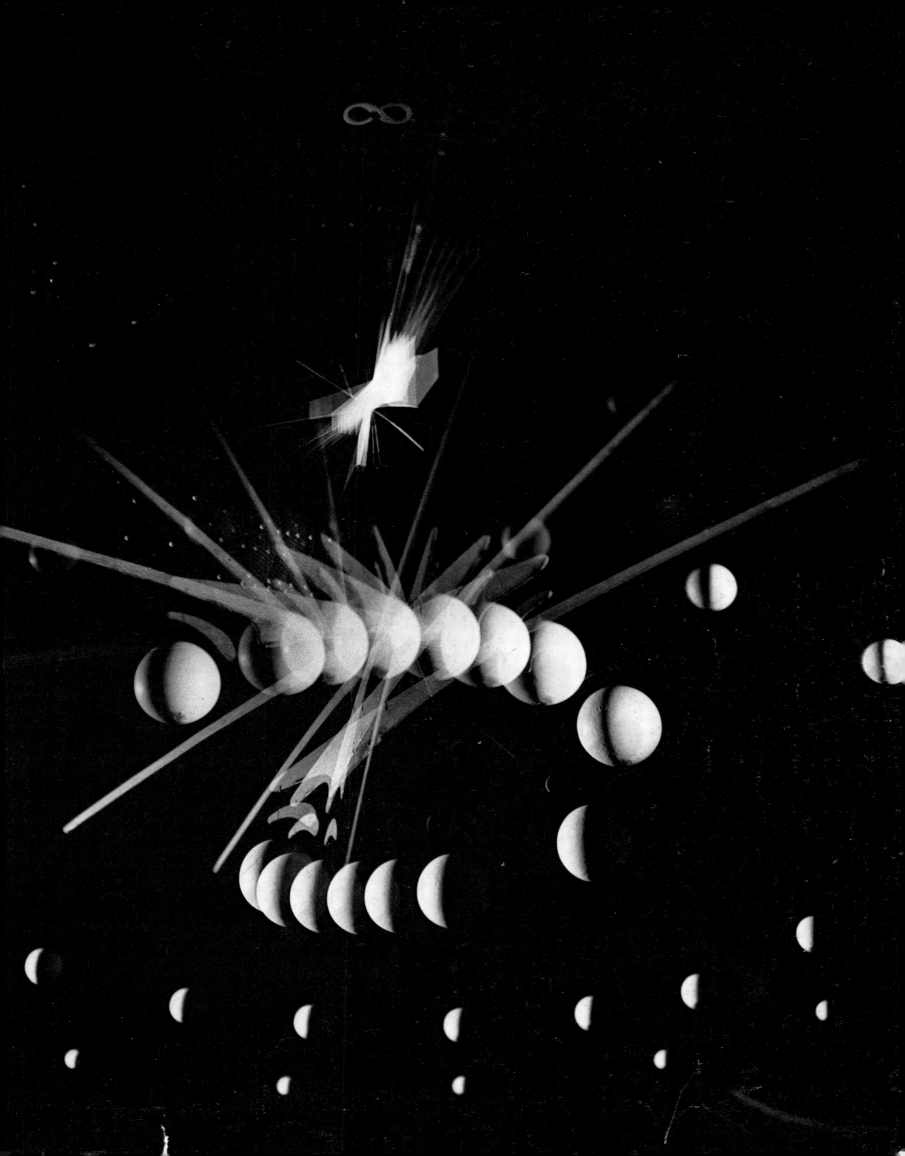

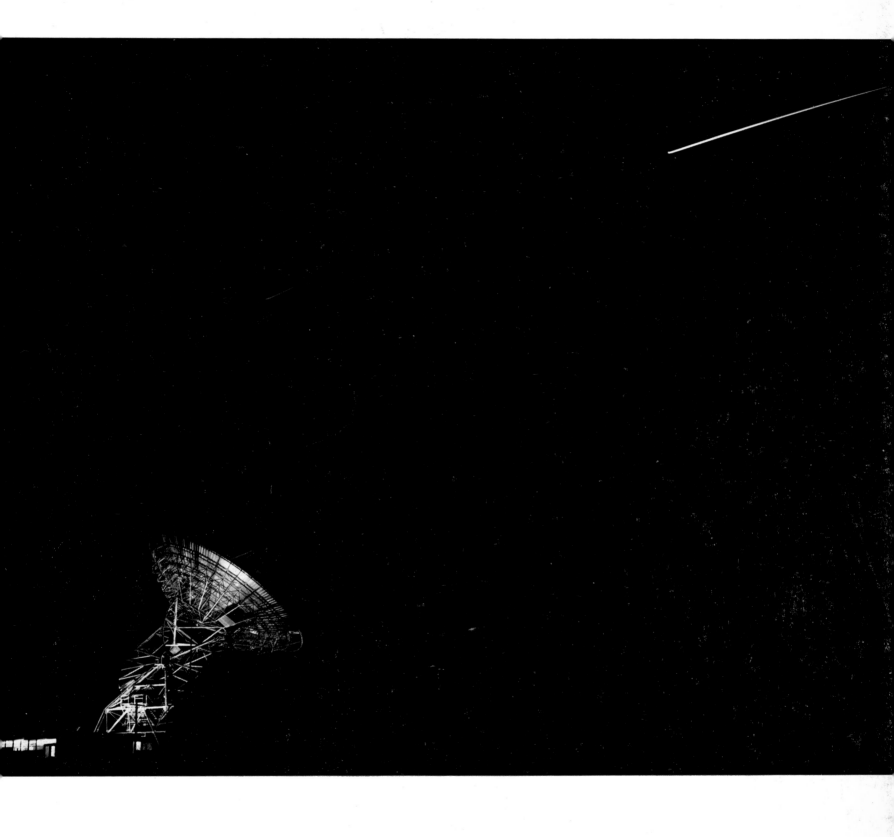

# X

*A Portfolio of North American Scenery*

Perhaps no other country possesses a greater wealth of scenic beauty and more varied landscapes—mountains and plains; rivers, lakes, and forests; deserts and cultivated lands—than the United States. I know the forty-eight states of the continental United States well, for I have traveled and photographed extensively in all of them for more than twenty years.

In the following portfolio are assembled fourteen photographs of views in the United States and one in Canada that to me seem particularly typical. This collection is, of course, severely restricted. The scope of the subject is so vast that it could not be covered in a thousand pictures. Some of the most famous and familiar sights are not included for the reason that they are so well-known and have been photographed so often and well; repeating them here would take space better used for photographs of things not seen before or not seen in such form.

Many of the following pictures are, as scenic photographs go, close-ups, showing the essence of an entire landscape in the form of a grain elevator, a farm, or a pair of railroad tracks. Some are in color, but only when color was of primary importance. Despite their limited number, these few photographs show an immense variety of scenery, ranging from the tidal flats of Maryland to the icy heights of the Rockies, from a lonely farm in Indiana to the stainless steel, bronze, and glass skyscrapers of New York. Together, they give at least an indication of the colossus that is America.

*112. Bench flume, Idaho*

An artificial river. Water is conducted from reservoirs high in the mountains to irrigate arable but normally waterless lowlands.

*113. Sunrise over the Grand Canyon, Arizona*

No photograph can truly convey the immensity of this view, the breathtaking hues—the shades of purple, pink, and red—and the silence.

*114. Dunes in Death Valley, California*

Here is the lowest point in the United States—282 feet below sea level—and the hottest.

*115. The Borego desert, California, in spring*

No one who has not seen it for himself would imagine that this seemingly sterile desert—a wasteland of sand and stone—could transform itself almost overnight into a lush garden where desert verbena, evening primrose, and a host of other flowering plants explode into a riot of color. And yet if the rain comes in time, this happens for a few weeks every spring.

*116. Pack horses on a glacier*

We were riding up Athabaska Glacier when we were caught by one of the sudden squalls that are so common in high mountains. Our horses, mountain-wise, had already turned away from the wind to wait out the storm. The next moment, the blizzard struck and blotted out everything—horses, mountains, and ice.

*117. Park Avenue, New York*

These are two of the more recent additions to New York's changing skyline. At the left is Mies van der Rohe's Seagram Building; at the right, the Lever Brothers Buildings by Skidmore, Owings and Merrill. Between the two, a part of

45

the General Electric Building on Lexington Avenue can be seen.

### 118/119. Transmission lines, Hoover Dam, Arizona-Nevada

Here are the hollow copper cables nearly 1½ inches in diameter that carry 287,000 volts to distant Los Angeles. The corona that surrounds these transmission lines is so powerful that my hair stood on end when I made this picture, and each time I touched the camera or tripod my fingertips drew tiny crackling sparks.

### 120. A walk in Magnolia Gardens, South Carolina

Thousands of spent magnolia blossoms had fallen from the surrounding trees to the brick-paved path, forming a magnificent, infinitely delicate, and fragrant carpet I was loath to tread upon.

### 121. Mosquito fighters working in a marsh

Man's eternal war against nature is waged here with poison sprays and gas masks but with questionable success.

### 122/123. Chesapeake Bay, Maryland

At sundown, with his limit of four ducks in the bag, a hunter pulls his decoys to the shore.

### 124. Railroad tracks in Nebraska

Shiny arrow-straight lines of silver converging at infinity symbolize the immensity of the midwestern plains. This was a lucky, unplanned shot—I happened to notice it as I was driving across a railroad overpass in Nebraska.

### 125. A Jupiter rocket and the moon

This picture was to have been a cover for *Life*, to celebrate the first rocket shot at the moon. But the Russians scooped the United States, and the photograph was never used. I made it at Huntsville, Alabama, with a Hasselblad on Ektachrome film. It is a double exposure: a 250-mm lens for the rocket, a 40-inch lens for the moon. I used this technique because the distance from the rocket was insufficient to permit use of my 40-inch telephoto lens, and if shot with the 250-mm lens the moon would have appeared ineffectively small.

### 126/127. A farm in Indiana

To me, this photograph has everything that the concept "farm" calls for: the hilltop site, the main house shaded by trees, the windmill rising above well-kept barns, and telephone wires paralleling the highway that connects homestead and town. The picture is one of a series of twenty-four I made for an assignment that called for a photograph of a typical midwestern farm. It took me two weeks to get it. I must have considered almost a hundred farms, many of them beautiful and photogenic. But either there was something missing—even if it was only a suitable place to put the camera—or there was something I didn't like—an ugly fence, a clump of shrubs—that spoiled an otherwise promising view. In making this particular photograph, I took about a dozen shots while cloud formations moved across the sky creating constantly shifting patterns of shadow and light. At times the farm was in sunshine, at times in shadow. But of all those pictures, this is the only one I felt captured the intangible rain-heavy mood that makes you feel the corn growing, which was what I sought.

### 128. A nunnery on the Hudson

The fading colors at summer's end provide a nostalgic setting for the faded elegance of what was once a Victorian mansion.

### 129. A grain elevator in Nebraska

Stout though badly cracked and patched, this grain elevator—symbol of the midwestern plains—has a pattern that might have inspired certain works of modern abstract art.

113 - 119 ▶

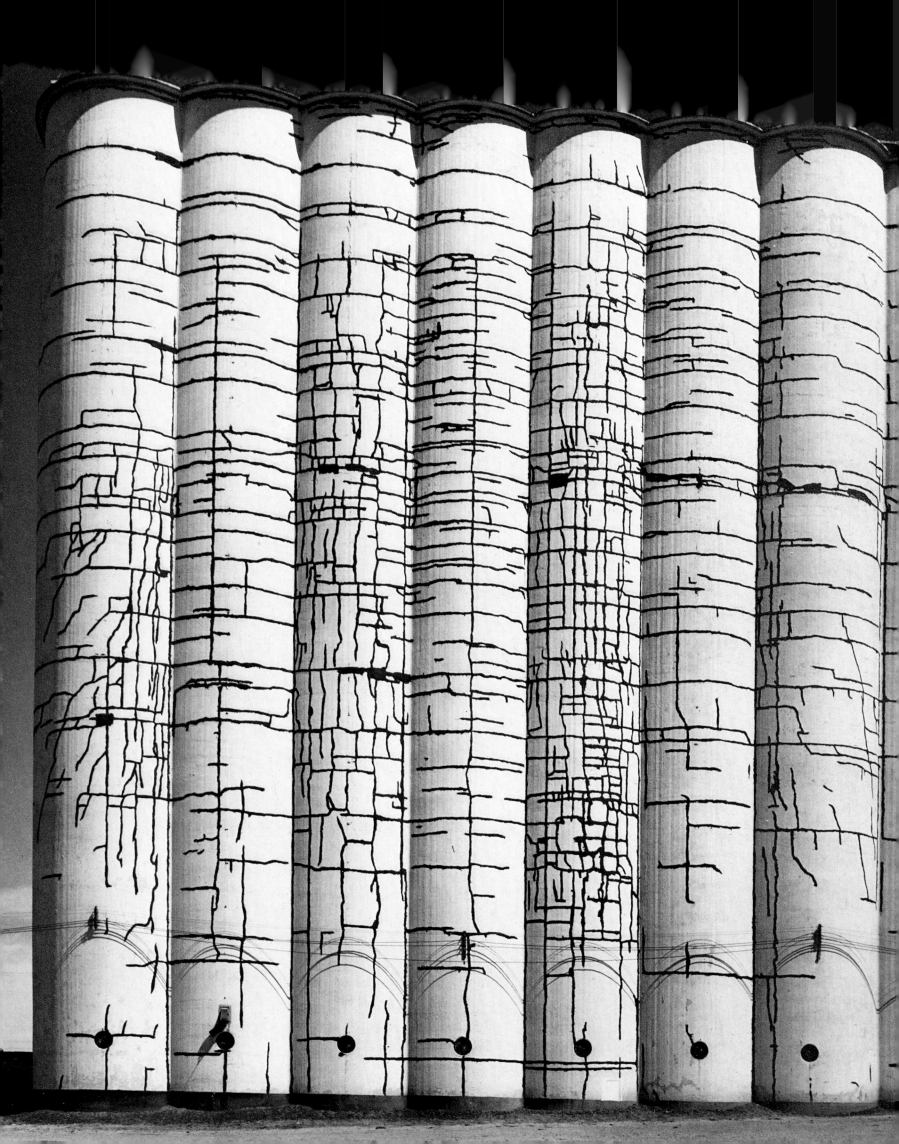

# XI

*Industry*

I have always been deeply interested in the construction of things and in their function—those created by nature and those made by man. Before I became a photographer I was, as I have already mentioned, an architect whose main interest was in structural engineering. Preoccupation with structures has, of course, had a great influence upon my photographic work, in which it is mainly manifested in subject selection: I am fascinated by—and like to photograph—whatever serves a functional purpose: the skeleton of an animal, the wing or feather of a bird, a bridge, a motor, or an electrical computer.... As a result, particularly during the forties in connection with the "war effort," I did a great deal of industrial work, photographing in steel mills, oil fields, uranium, copper, mercury, and coal mines, and plants manufacturing airplanes, guns, engines of various kinds, automobiles, electric motors and generators, locomotives, explosives, electronic computers, television sets, plastics, glass, and many other products.

In photographing for industry, a photographer is confronted with a special set of problems. It is heavy, often dirty, and sometimes dangerous work; a wrong step or a moment of inattention can lead to serious injury or death. Working conditions generally range from the difficult to the impossible. That conditions are usually so poor is mainly due to the fact that a photographer must never interrupt production, and in avoiding this his own work of camera placement, arrangement of subjects to be photographed (composition), and illumination naturally becomes more difficult. Furthermore, there is the pressure of time. And in addition, for anyone unfamiliar with industrial operations, there is the first and often continuing impression of hopeless confusion, clutter, dirt, noise, and harsh, unphotogenic light to work against.

Creating order out of this apparent chaos by separating important aspects from nonessential, obscuring details, and presenting the subject in graphically attractive form, is of course the aim of the industrial photographer. Where the eye is blinded in reality, the ear deafened, and the mind confused, the camera creates order and definite impressions emerge—images of glistening precision-shaped forms; of fire, heat, and light; of action and accomplishment.

*130. Color research lab of the Agfa, Leverkusen, Germany*

The shapes and colors in this photograph suggest to me all the beauty and magic of modern chemistry.

*131. Still life: Bayer Farbenfabriken A. G., Leverkusen, Germany*

I found this purplish oxidized pan on a junk pile in one of the oldest sections of the Bayer works. Its jewel-like beauty seemed to me sufficient reason to photograph it.

*132. American Locomotive Co., Schenectady, New York*

These 0-8-0 locomotives undergoing final assembly on the erecting floor were part of a lend-lease shipment destined for Russia during the last war.

*133. Plexiglass nose cone for an airplane*

The sheer beauty of this precisely curved functional form provides an aesthetic experience.

*134/135. SAGE operation center*

This is one of the centers of the United States system of defense against enemy attack, in which giant electronic computers make split-second decisions and, upon demand from the airmen, instantly display on TV-like screens any of thousands of items of memorized data assembled from the incoming reports of radar and ground observation. Capturing the weird atmosphere on Ektachrome daylight film required a 10-minute exposure at *f*/6.3. I used a 5×7-inch Linhof Technika equipped with a 21-cm Zeiss Tessar *f*/6.3, making use of the camera's swings and tilts to extend the zone of sharpness in depth.

*136. Glass cloth weaving, Owens-Corning,*
        *Newark, Ohio*
*137. Crankshaft inspection, Pratt & Whitney Co.,*
        *Hartford, Connecticut*

In my opinion, the most important requirement for a successful picture of this kind is the effective rendering of the marvelous shapes and textures of the subject by means of a combination of sharpness and the right illumination. This type of photograph is worthless unless one can virtually feel the different kinds of surfaces—the silky smoothness of the fiberglass strands, the oily hardness of the highly polished steel.

*138. Bar mill, Jones and Laughlin, Pittsburgh,*
        *Pennsylvania*

In this ultramodern, fully automated mill, the entire process from roughing to finishing takes only 18 seconds, the steel traveling at almost 40 miles per hour. Only a color photograph can convey the full beauty of this operation, which lies in the color contrast between the cool, blue-green light of the mercury-vapor lamps and the fiery redness of the steel.

*139. B-36 bomber assembly line*

This is one of the gigantic plants where U.S. bombers were turned out on an assembly-line schedule during the last war. After seeing the immensity of this effort devoted to destruction, it seems to me no thinking person can help but question the sanity of people all over the world.

*140/141. Ship propeller shop, Bethlehem Steel Co.*

*Left:* Pattern shop. Propeller patterns are built up in layer by layer of wood. *Center:* Foundry. Pouring of the molten manganese-bronze into the mold has just been completed. *Right:* Finishing shop. Propellers are calibrated to the correct pitch at all radii, and balanced. The precise curves of these propellers—forms determined strictly by their function—are a source of aesthetic pleasure.

*142. Crankshaft forging, Wyman-Gordon,*
        *Harvey, Illinois*

To capture the heart of this operation—the pounding of the massive hammer's downward beat—I timed my exposure to produce a carefully calculated degree of motion-symbolizing blur.

*143. Pouring ingots, U.S. Steel plant, Pittsburgh,*
        *Pennsylvania*

Perhaps the most dramatic of all industrial operations is "teeming"—the process of pouring molten steel from ladles holding up to 200 tons, into molds to produce ingots. As soon as the plug is pulled, the steel begins to flow and the entire enormous shed explodes into a glare brighter than a dozen suns that radiates unbearable heat. Only the most intense contrast of black and white combined with halation can transfer to a photograph the drama of this unforgettable spectacle.

# XII

*American Cities*

For me, a former architect, the cities of the United States have always held a unique fascination. Years before I came to America, I dreamed of someday making a picture book of New York, which, known to me then only through photographs and descriptions, seemed the most fabulous place on earth. That dream was twice realized: the first time in *New York,* a large book containing 96 pages of pictures; and the second time in *The Face of New York* (now in its fifth printing). This is a correlation of pictures of the old city and the new—my own photographs shown in juxtaposition to old lithographs and pictures of New York.

In the course of my work for *Life* I have been in all the larger cities of the United States and a great many of the smaller ones. What struck me forcibly was the lack of planning evident in them. Although Americans are the greatest of organizers, and although business, advertising campaigns, and political ventures are carefully researched and planned with knowledge and care down to the smallest detail, the towns and cities of the United States begin and expand in a disorganized way, with everyone taking as much advantage as possible for himself and having little or no regard for the welfare of the community. Planning is not only neglected but actually opposed by many influential people, who regard it as "government interference," although as a rule they are the first to demand government aid when it is to their own benefit or to offset the consequences of their own selfishness and greed. The result of this quite common attitude is, of course, the haphazard growth-pattern typical of many American cities: an inner core, the "downtown" area, which is usually made up of a jumble of modern skyscrapers, nondescript shopping streets, blighted blocks, and vacant lots; a suburban belt of "developments" or "subdivisions," shopping centers, and reasonably modern, though usually unbelievably monotonous, private homes; and strips of gaudy or shoddy small enterprises, gas stations, used car lots, junk yards, hamburger stands, and flashy motels paralleling and blighting the more important access roads to the town.

I made the following pictures to convey specific impressions of particular cities. Some of them were made with standard equipment; others, with extreme telephoto lenses because only such lenses could convey the intense feelings the subjects evoke. In making these photographs I was not out to make sensational pictures but to report objectively on sensational subjects, and thus give the reader freedom to make his own evaluation.

*144. The Empire State Building, New York*

This is the world's tallest building, but it does not appear to be so when seen from the street partly obscured by much smaller structures. To show it in its incredible height, I had to photograph it from a distance of seven miles with a 40-inch super telephoto lens. By putting a few miles of New Jersey marsh, the town of Weehawken, the Hudson River (invisible behind the ridge), and half of Manhattan between the camera and the building, I overcame the effect of diminution and was able to show this fantastic skyscraper in almost true proportions in relation to its surroundings.

## 145. Betatakin, Navajo National Monument, Arizona

These are some of the oldest remains of an American city. Approximately 700 years old, the Indian ruins cling to the walls and hug the sloping floor of an immense cave in the side of a red sandstone cliff that forms the sheer, 500-foot-high wall of a canyon almost 100 miles from the nearest paved road.

## 146/147. New Orleans, Louisiana

This is one of the least typical American cities. Its tempo is almost leisurely, reflecting its French heritage. To express its Old World atmosphere, I framed this view in the wrought-iron grillwork of a balcony, which is characteristic of New Orleans and suggests its elegance, beauty, and gracious living.

## 148/149. Chicago, Illinois

Originally called the Golden Flats, this tenement built in 1894 is as good an example as any of the infamous Chicago slums, which, perhaps, are the worst slums anywhere. Through slum-clearance projects, many of the most blighted blocks have by now been razed. Gleaming new structures of concrete and glass are being erected in their place —tall, lofty buildings widely spaced, separated by playgrounds, lawns, and trees, and open to the fresh clean air from the lake.

## 150/151. Houston, Texas

I made this photograph at a time when Houston was in an explosive building boom, which I tried to express symbolically by photographing buildings and construction work through the framework of a scaffold at the site of a new hospital. Not long after I made this picture, the corner lot occupied by the little church was sold to developing interests for a reported cost of $2,000 per inch of street frontage; it is now the site of another skyscraper. Such ruthless exploitation of limited space, unless offset by wise planning, will in time defeat its own purpose and choke our cities to death.

## 152/153. Van Nuys Gardens, California

To me, a development like this, which is typical of hundreds of others throughout the country, is one of the horrors of our age. Its ugliness, monotony, and shoddiness, its disregard for all aesthetic values—exemplified by its complete lack of trees (but overabundance of light and telephone poles) —are the inevitable result of exploitation and greed and the evidence of a colossal contempt for people.

## 154/155. Fifth Avenue, New York

This picture was taken on a beautiful day in spring, but here the beauty of spring is nowhere apparent. I feel that it well symbolizes man's being choked by his own creation.

## 156/157. The liner "Queen Mary" passing 42nd Street, New York

One of the world's biggest ships seen against the background of one of the world's largest cities. In this photograph I tried to capture something of the stimulating and exhilarating atmosphere that permeates New York. Its ugliness and inhuman aspects cannot negate the fact that its aggregate of museums and art galleries, universities and research institutions, libraries, theatres, and concert halls makes it the intellectual, cultural, and scientific focus of the world. Almost everyone coming from or going to Europe—passing between the Old World and the new—goes through New York and in passing enriches the city.

## 158/159. Coney Island beach, New York

Mass-production, mass-communication, mass-appeal, etc., is brought to mind by this photograph, which shows New Yorkers enjoying Sunday at the beach. On such beaches, the densest crowds are invariably near the subway exits or parking lots; a few hundred feet away the beach is less crowded, and half a mile away it is virtually empty. In the automobile age people are loath to walk.

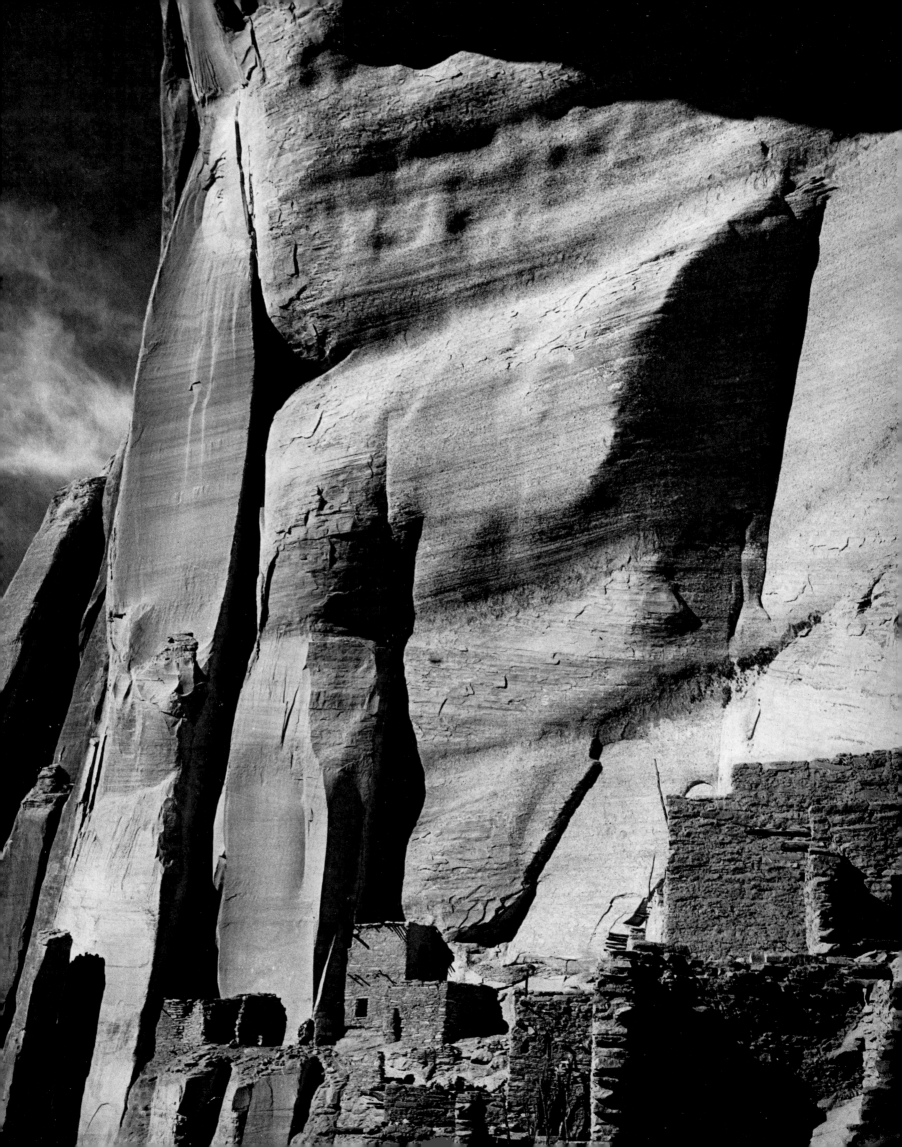

# XIII

## Forms of Nature

I have always been attracted by all the different forms of nature, being particularly interested in the structural aspects of animals and plants. I have looked at and studied them, not from the point of view of the artist, but from that of the architect and engineer, whose main concern is with structure, construction, and function. In studying a flower, bone, feather, wing, an insect eye, snail shell, or other creation of nature, I find beauty of the highest possible level.

This kind of beauty is totally divorced from the common concept of beauty as ornament or decoration—a means of embellishing or disguising underlying structure. What I am talking about here is the inherent universal beauty that results from the perfect fusion of purpose, function and form.

We have just begun to "discover" and to appreciate this true kind of beauty—the beauty of functional form—which, in the works of man, we see in the sleek shapes of jet planes, the parabolic curves of a suspension bridge, the shapes of modern microscopes and other scientific instruments, optical products, laboratory glassware, surgical instruments, and numerous objects whose function-given shapes have not yet been corrupted by "stylists." This kind of beauty, which is still rare in man's work, is found everywhere in nature.

Nature's forms, as opposed to most forms created by man, are functional. They were evolved through necessity, and those that did not function well enough did not survive. Some that at first functioned poorly gradually grew more perfect. For example, the wings of the earliest known birdlike creature, *Archeopteryx*, were clumsy and doubtless much limited in function when compared to the more highly developed—and consequently far more beautiful—wings of the present-day hawks. Think of the skeletons of vertebrates: they are marvels of functional engineering, combining the rigidity needed to support the weight of the animal, with the flexibility and delicate articulation needed to enable it to move, function, and live. They combine maximum strength with minimum weight and expenditure of material. Each bone is exquisitely shaped, finished more perfectly than a sculpture by Brancusi or Rivera, its beauty that of perfect functional form, its function reflected in its shape: tubular bones for support, flat bones for protection like armor plate, the motion-providing ball-and-socket joint of the hip, light and hollow bones for fleet and flying animals, dense and heavy bones for slow and heavy animals and swimmers. The same basic principles are found in all other forms of nature. Thus, a flower's beauty is not ornamental or aesthetic but functional, designed to aid propagation. To me, this realization does not diminish the enjoyment of flowers but rather deepens it by relating their beauty to the mystery of birth, growth, and death—the cycle which science can describe but cannot explain, just as it can precisely measure the frequencies of the electromagnetic radiations we perceive as colors but cannot explain how color sensations are produced within the brain. Nor can science explain the psychological effects of color, or why we enjoy color harmonies, or color in works of art. We all know that understanding, though it may add another dimension of interest, is not necessary to enjoyment. Few people understand the physics of color, but almost everyone is moved by the colors of a sunset. It is in this way—through feeling and sensitivity—that most of us respond to the beauty of nature's functional forms, perhaps at times aware of meaning beyond the beauty, but not primarily concerned with it.

### 160. Sand pattern

Wind and gravity produced this beautiful design, which I photographed in California's Death Valley. Although such a graph of force and time may be marred by footprints or destroyed, it will soon be sculptured again by winds and gravity, eternally.

### 161. Sectionalized shell of a nautilus
### 161a. Part of the spinal column of a skate

No artist could improve the beauty, no craftsman match the perfection of execution, of these structures that grew in accordance with inherited patterns going back to the beginnings of time.

### 162/163. Shells of different mollusks

The variety of the forms of nature is unlimited, their number infinite. These four photographs show four different solutions to the protective needs of certain mollusks. Each shell evolved to provide maximum protection in accordance with the specific environment and way of life of the respective mollusk, the different requirements being reflected in the differences in design: corrugated, ribbed, or spherical surface; presence or absence of protective spines; thinness or thickness of the walls.

### 164/165. Three different skeletons

A large number of organisms depend for support upon a skeleton, which, if external—as in the case of insects, crabs, mollusks, starfish, and others—simultaneously serves as a protection. Here are three different types of skeleton: (Left) The woody skeleton of a Cholla cactus is a rigid, tubular, girder-like structure, unbelievably light yet unbelievably strong. (Center) The protective shell of a clam, its broken form revealing its layered, corrugated structure. (Right) The skeleton of a Gaboon viper, infinitely delicate, beautifully articulate, is flexible, elastic, and almost unbreakable. Each serves its possessor's needs perfectly.

### 166. Tendril of a passion flower

Resembling a powerful spring, the form of the tendril indicates its tenacious force, which never releases its grip. It will break under strain before it loosens.

### 167. Skull of the crucifix catfish

The strong, reinforcing bone ridges and braces that form a cross gave this fish its name.

### 168/169. Bat flight

This is the entrance of a limestone cave near New Braunfels, Texas, which is the home of some eight million bats. At nightfall, the bats emerge, first one, then another. Then a small band appears in the sunken entrance of the cave. They fly in circles that swell to tens of thousands, to millions, of small flapping forms that quickly fill the shallow bowl in front of the cave like a storm of black snow, as each bat, as if riding an immense carousel, swings around in three circles and flies away.

### 170. Nest of the mud-dauber wasp
### 171. Sectionalized anthill

Man is not the world's only architect and engineer. Many animals build elaborate structures—the dams and flood-control projects of the beaver, the often unbelievably skillfully built nests of birds, the underground labyrinths of the mole, the towering cities of ants and tropical termites, the intricate hanging nests of wasps, the webs and snares of spiders. Here the clay tubes that a species of wasp builds as protection for its eggs, and the interior of an anthill, are shown. Considering the sizes and resources of their builders, both structures command respect.

### 172. Soaring turkey vulture

This seems to me the ultimate joy of life: to be able to escape the pull of gravity, to soar in effortless flight, to ride like this bird of prey the columns of rising air, gliding, floating, spiraling in shimmering light.

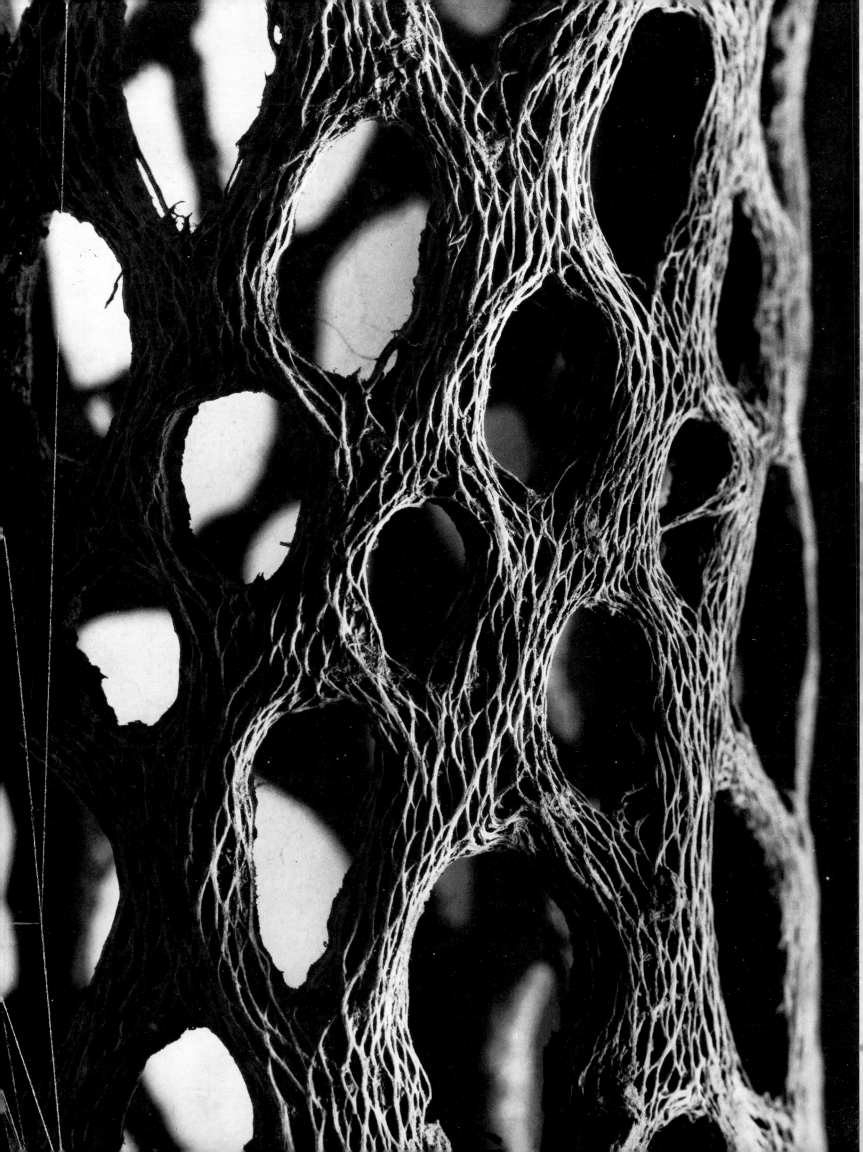

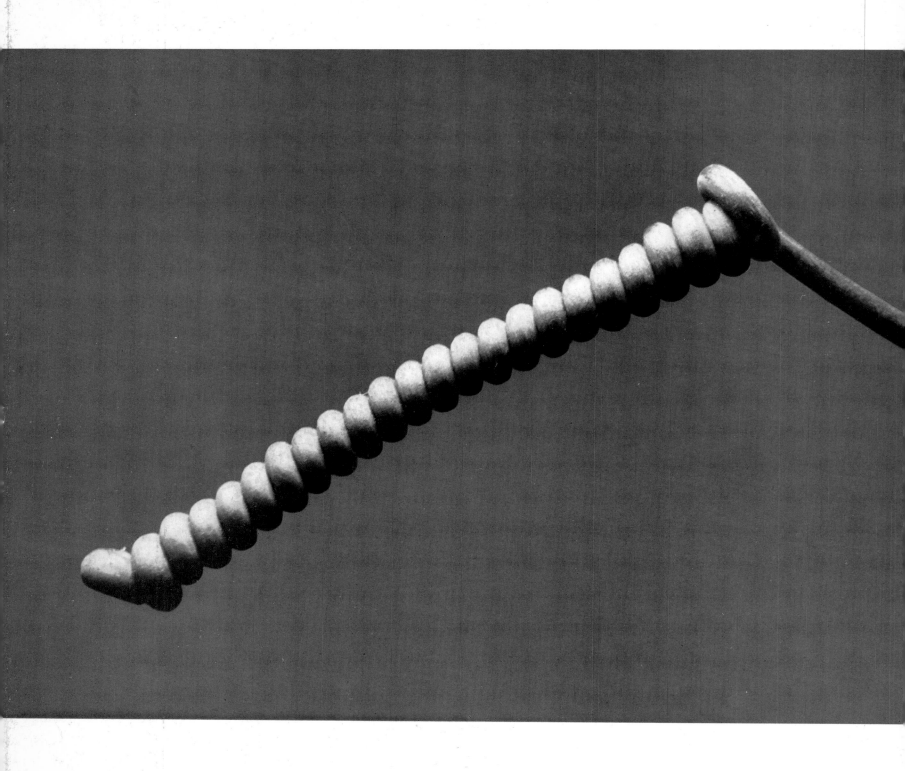

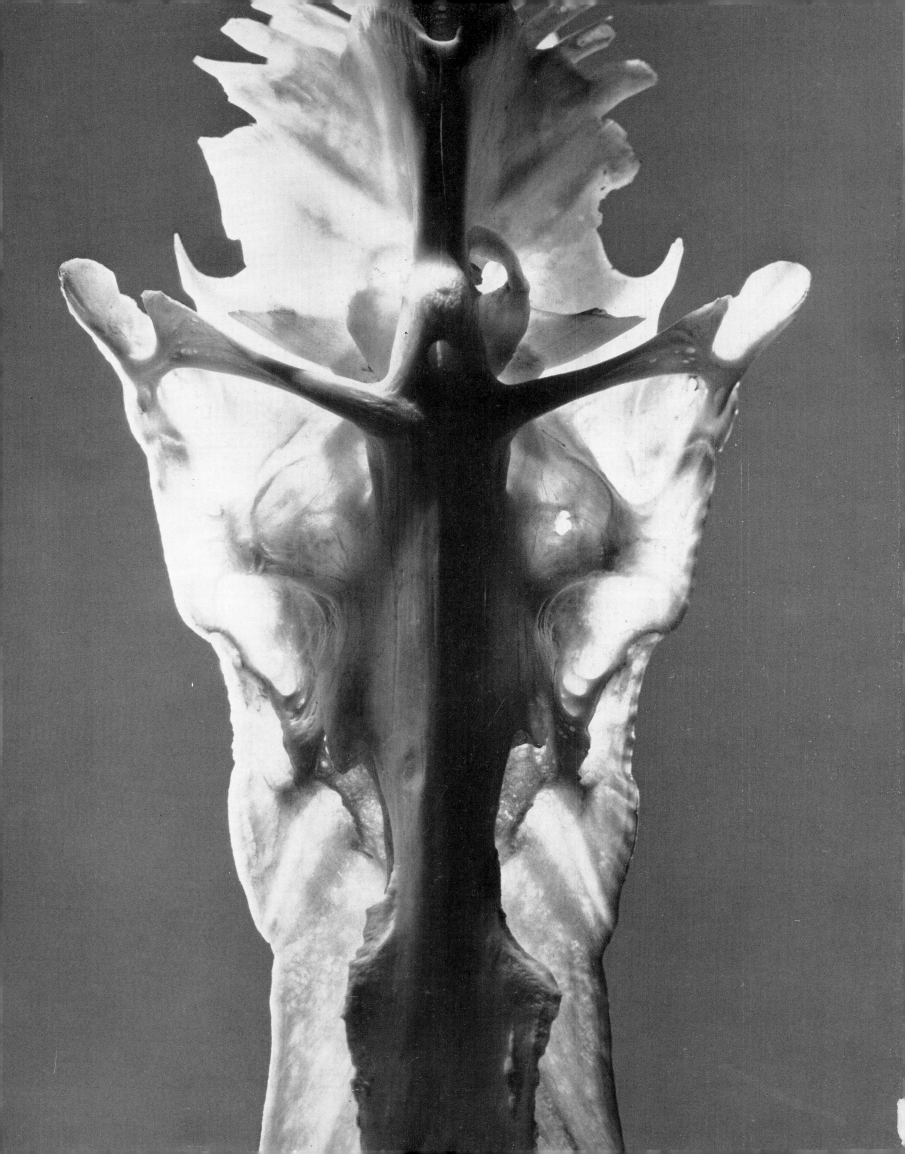

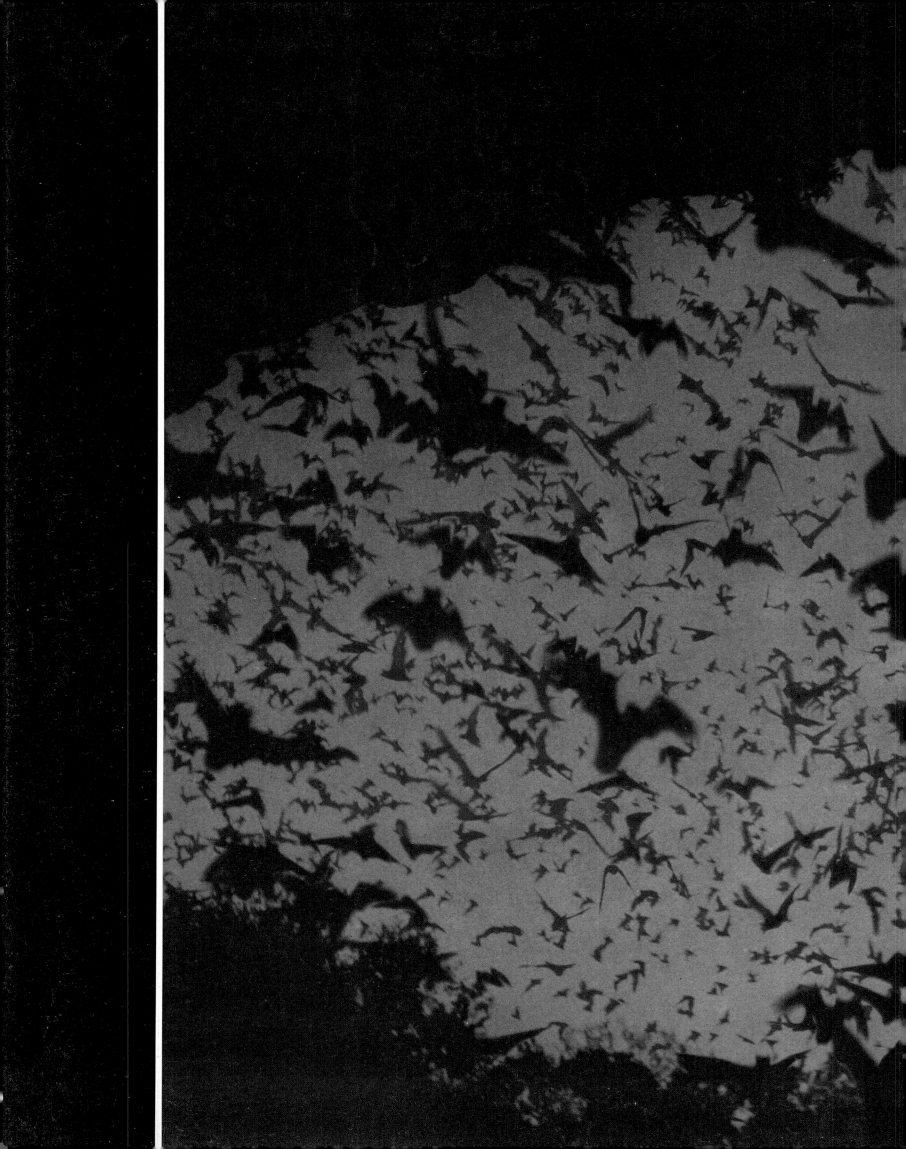